RESEARCH
METHODS *for*
EVIDENCE-BASED
PRACTICE

This book is dedicated to Professor Albert R. Roberts. He and I discussed this edition of the books previously titled

Wodarski, J. S. (1981). Role of research in clinical practice. *Baltimore, MD: University Park Press.*

Wodarski, J. S. (1997). Research methods for clinical social workers: Empirical practice. *New York: Springer.*

It was through Al's coaching that this book started. Unfortunately, after two chapters were written, Al passed away on June 23, 2008. I dedicate this book to Al, whom I met in 1976 when I was teaching at the University of Maryland. Al was a dedicated student who took many courses from me, and I also served as his dissertation advisor. He helped a tremendous number of people in a scholarly way. We had many weekly talks about the profession and where it was going. It was an honor to have "Big Al" as a student and as one of my esteemed colleagues, and I will miss him tremendously.

—J. S. W.

RESEARCH METHODS *for* EVIDENCE-BASED PRACTICE

JOHN S. WODARSKI
The University of Tennessee

LAURA M. HOPSON
University at Albany, State University of New York

 EVIDENCE-BASED PRACTICE IN SOCIAL WORK

Los Angeles | London | New Delhi
Singapore | Washington DC

Los Angeles | London | New Delhi
Singapore | Washington DC

FOR INFORMATION

SAGE Publications, Inc.
2455 Teller Road
Thousand Oaks, California 91320
E-mail: order@sagepub.com

SAGE Publications Ltd.
1 Oliver's Yard
55 City Road
London, EC1Y 1SP
United Kingdom

SAGE Publications India Pvt. Ltd.
B 1/I 1 Mohan Cooperative Industrial Area
Mathura Road, New Delhi 110 044
India

SAGE Publications Asia-Pacific Pte. Ltd.
33 Pekin Street #02-01
Far East Square
Singapore 048763

Acquisitions Editor: Kassie Graves
Editorial Assistant: Courtney Munz
Production Editor: Karen Wiley
Copy Editor: Megan Granger
Typesetter: Hurix Systems Pvt. Ltd.
Proofreader: Laura Webb
Indexer: Jeanne Busemeyer
Cover Designer: Candice Harman
Marketing Manager: Katie Winter
Permissions Editor: Adele Hutchinson

Printed in the United States of America.

Library of Congress Cataloging-in-Publication Data

Wodarski, John S.
Research methods for evidence-based practice / John Wodarski, Laura M. Hopson.

p. cm.—(Evidence-based practice in the human services)
Includes bibliographical references and index.

ISBN 978-1-4129-9098-1 (pbk.)

1. Social service—Research. 2. Evidence-based social work. I. Hopson, Laura M. II. Title.

HV11.W698 2012

361.3072—dc23

2011027823

This book is printed on acid-free paper.

11 12 13 14 15 10 9 8 7 6 5 4 3 2 1

Contents

Preface

Within the past four decades, the social work profession has responded to the challenge to base practice on empirical evidence to adequately meet client needs. Most social workers would agree that the challenge has resulted in positive changes in the majority of cases—for example, in the execution of relevant research studies; the incorporation of more research findings into practice; the development of a technology of interpersonal helping; an emphasis on the incorporation of new knowledge bases, such as sociobehavioral and systems theory, in the curricula of schools of social work; and the development of services to meet emerging client needs and evidence-based practice (Dulmus & Wodarski, 1996; Fraser, 1994; Roberts & Yeager, 2004; Thyer & Myers, 2007; Thyer & Wodarski, 2007; Wodarski, Thyer, Iodice, & Pinkston, 1991).

A past allegation about practice methods' lack of effectiveness is no longer relevant with the accumulation of substantial empirical bases from many interpersonal helping strategies (Ammerman & Hersen, 1995; Wodarski, 2009). However, the continued minimal use of empirical methods to evaluate practice and the limited incorporation of relevant behavioral science knowledge in practice models are deficiencies of the profession. One of the ingenious proposals to meet this challenge is to train practitioners who can evaluate knowledge produced in the behavioral sciences and who, in turn, can translate such knowledge into practice principles (Bloom & Fischer, 1982; Briggs & Rzepnicki, 2004; Gambrill, 1990; Wodarski, Feit, & Green, 1995). Along those lines, this book proposes that bachelor's-level practitioners should be consumers of knowledge that facilitates effective practice; that master's-level practitioners should be sophisticated practitioners or managers, or both; and that doctoral-level practitioners should be producers and evaluators of knowledge.

In response to the call for empirically based practice, increased emphasis on research in practice has developed—that is, the use of evaluative research to provide a rational basis for the delivery of services (Alter & Evans, 1990). This volume aims to help practitioners understand the research process and equip them with the necessary tools and skills to (a) evaluate studies, (b) translate relevant behavioral science knowledge into practice principles, and (c) implement evaluation procedures in their daily practice.

The scientific approach to social work practice offers much promise for the profession. Based on empirical data and scientific findings, it makes available concrete tools for effective intervention and, most important, builds into the intervention process a problem-solving and evaluative component needed in social work practice. The chapters that follow discuss how clinical social workers can incorporate research methodology into their practicing repertoires. Chapter 2 covers the use of scientific and practice criteria to evaluate the relevance of behavioral science knowledge and empirical studies for social work practice. Chapter 3 reviews the use of behavioral science knowledge to create therapeutic services in terms of answering the questions of implementation of change strategy (i.e., where, by whom, why, for how long, on what level, and relapse-prevention procedures). Chapter 4 reviews practical aspects of doing research. Chapter 5 covers operationalizing outcome concepts and choosing appropriate measures to be used in evaluating practice. Chapters 6 and 7 discuss building adequate studies through the use of appropriate designs. Chapter 8 describes the statistical procedures necessary for deciding whether a treatment significantly improved clients' functioning. Chapter 9 reviews complex multivariate statistics. Chapter 10 discusses the use of Management Information Systems and computer-based measures. Chapter 11 demonstrates how grants facilitate the evaluation of effective social work services and provides guidelines for preparing grant applications. Chapter 12 discusses emerging trends and issues related to evidence-based practice.

REFERENCES

Alter, C., & Evans, W. (1990). *Evaluating your practice: A guide to self-assessment.* New York: Springer.

Ammerman, R. T., & Hersen, M. (1995). *Handbook of child behavior therapy.* New York: Wiley.

Bloom, M., & Fischer, J. (1982). *Evaluating practice: Guidelines for the accountable professional.* Englewood Cliffs, NJ: Prentice Hall.

Briggs, H. E., & Rzepnicki, T. L. (Eds.). (2004). *Using evidence in social work practice: Behavioral perspectives.* Chicago: Lyceum.

Dulmus, C. N., & Wodarski, J. S. (1996). Assessment and effective treatments of childhood psychopathology: Responsibilities and implications for practice. *Journal of Child and Adolescent Group Therapy, 6*(2), 75–99.

Fraser, M. W. (1994, Spring/Summer). Scholarship and research in social work: Emerging challenges. *Journal of Social Work Education, 30,* 252–266.

Gambrill, E. (1990). *Critical thinking in clinical practice.* San Francisco: Jossey-Bass.

Roberts, A. R., & Yeager, K. R. (2004). *Evidence-based practice manual: Research and outcome measures in health and human services.* New York: Oxford University Press.

Thyer, B. A., & Myers, L. L. (2007). *A social worker's guide to evaluating practice outcomes.* Alexandria, VA: CSWE Press.

Thyer, B. A., & Wodarski, J. S. (Eds.). (2007). *Social work in mental health: An evidenced-based approach.* Hoboken, NJ: Wiley.

Wodarski, J. S. (2009). *Behavioral medicine: A social worker's guide.* New York: Routledge.

Wodarski, J. S., Feit, M. D., & Green, R. K. (1995). Graduate social work education: A review of two decades of empirical research and considerations for the future. *Social Service Review, 69,* 108–130.

Wodarski, J. S., Thyer, B. A., Iodice, J. D., & Pinkston, R. (1991). Graduate social work education: A review of empirical research. *Journal of Social Service Research, 14*(314), 23–44.

CHAPTER 1

Evidence-Based Practice

An Introduction

RATIONALE FOR THE EMPIRICAL PRACTITIONER

The incorporation into social work practice of research methods and practice models based on behavioral science knowledge has increased during the past four decades. A primary reason for this move is the accumulating evidence that indicates the substantial effectiveness of empirically based interpersonal helping methods (Mullen, Bledsoe, & Bellamy, 2008; Thyer & Wodarski, 2007). Likewise, practitioners have access to tools that allow for evaluating the effectiveness of their practice, including reliable and valid measurement instruments that help obtain consistent and accurate measures of the presenting problem (Bloom, Fischer, & Orme, 2009). Another positive trend is the provision by federal agencies of adequate funding for evaluating empirical practice interventions on a broad scale. The field is ready to employ the necessary sophisticated designs to evaluate traditional services adequately and identify those interventions that need further refinement.

A concurrent positive development during this transitional period has been the profession's increasing commitment to base decisions on scientific principles and research data rather than solely on theoretical tradition and practice authority. However, we have yet to develop formal professional development opportunities to adequately train social work practitioners in evidence-based practice methods. This professional development will need to include an emphasis on setting specific, measureable goals, integrating information about current research with knowledge of client values and needs, implementing research-based practices, and evaluating the effectiveness of these practices.

Increased external pressures at the federal and state levels and from professional organizations for accountability in social work practice are providing an additional incentive for using evidence-based practice. In addition, social workers and other professionals working without empirically based practices are at risk for increased malpractice suits. Society has begun to demand proof that interventions work (Howard, Himle, Jenson, & Vaughn, 2009). Clinicians are not the only ones being held responsible for professional behavior. Universities have been challenged over their role in educating incompetent practitioners. In Louisiana, a client successfully sued her therapist and was awarded $1.7 million. The therapist was a graduate of an education program with an emphasis in counseling in Louisiana Tech's College of Education. A lawsuit was also filed against the college for inadequately preparing this graduate (Custer, 1994). Is academia adequately preparing students to enter the field as mental health clinicians? In referring to social work master's programs, Hepler and Noble (1990) state, "The quality of social work education ultimately affects practice competence and the social welfare of citizens" (p. 126). Where, then, does responsibility end for the school and rest with the graduate who is now a practitioner?

Managed care companies are also putting pressure on social workers and other mental health professionals to produce empirical treatment with proven outcomes. Managed care is an inescapable element of mental health services in America today (Long, Homesley, & Wodarski, 2007). Thyer (1995) states,

> To the extent that a service provider can produce evidence that the services he or she will be providing to children are well-supported by sound clinical research studies, authorization for such treatments is enhanced. If managed care programs produce incentives to select demonstrable effective treatments, where these are known to exist, this will be to the benefit of the profession and our child clients. (p. 81)

As third parties make decisions regarding reimbursement to clients for treatment, practitioners will be forced to demonstrate outcomes based on treatment.

WHAT IS EVIDENCE-BASED PRACTICE?

Evidence-based practice is often described as a process in which practitioners integrate information about client needs and values with knowledge of research on effective interventions (Gambrill, 2003; Gambrill, 2006; Sackett, Straus, Richardson, Rosenberg, & Haynes, 2000). Gambrill (2006) outlines the following steps in conducting evidence-based practice, which were originally articulated by Sackett et al. (2000):

1. *Construct well-structured answerable questions that will guide practice decisions.* Creating specific questions based on information provided during the assessment process will help practitioners and clients define the primary presenting problem and choose an appropriate intervention strategy. An example of a well-structured answerable question is, "Will my client's anxiety symptoms be reduced by participation in weekly cognitive behavioral therapy sessions?"

2. *Find the best available evidence with which to answer these questions.* Clinicians have access to a number of online resources for finding information on evidence-based practices. Many federal funders of social service programs provide a list of the interventions they consider to be evidence based. Such lists are available through the National Registry of Effective Programs and Practices, the National Institute of Drug Abuse, the Office of Juvenile Justice and Delinquency Prevention, the Centers for Disease Control and Prevention, and other federal organizations. A list of web resources is provided at the

end of the chapter. University libraries typically provide online access to current research articles for students, but practitioners who are not affiliated with a university are unlikely to have access to these resources.

3. *Apply critical thinking in analyzing the evidence for its validity, impact on client outcomes, and applicability for practice settings.* Although practitioners are limited in the amount of time they can devote to reading research articles, it is important to examine studies for the size of the effect on client outcomes. Practitioners also need the skills to evaluate whether something other than the intervention evaluated may be responsible for their outcomes. This information is invaluable in determining whether the researcher's conclusions are justified and the intervention is likely to be helpful to your client.

4. *Use this critical analysis of the research to guide practice decisions.* This includes deciding whether the intervention is relevant for your client and his or her presenting problem given the existing research support and considering client values and preferences.

5. *Evaluate the effectiveness of the intervention with your unique clients within your practice settings.* Even interventions with solid research support need to be evaluated with your clients. The client populations, settings, and clinicians participating in research studies may differ from those in your setting, and the intervention may affect your clients differently. Therefore, systematically measuring your clients' progress toward achieving their desired outcomes is important even when the intervention has been shown to be effective with other clients.

THE IMPORTANCE OF CRITICAL THINKING FOR EVIDENCE-BASED PRACTICE

Because social workers must integrate multiple perspectives and sources of information, critical thinking becomes a prerequisite for engaging in evidence-based practice. Critical thinking involves weighing multiple perspectives, evaluating the evidence provided, and considering alternative explanations before making a decision. In social work practice, this includes analyzing the state of the research evidence. When evaluating the quality of research findings, practitioners can focus on eight guiding questions for invoking critical thinking in the examination of various theories of practice:

1.   What is the issue or claim being made in simple and direct language?

2.   Are there any ambiguities or a lack of clarity in the claim?

3.   What are the underlying value and theory assumptions?

4.   Is there indication of any misleading beliefs or faulty reasoning?

5.   How good is the evidence presented?

6.   Is any important information missing?

7.   Is consideration given to alternative explanations?

8.   Are the conclusions reasonable?

Taking critical thinking a step further, social workers will need to weigh their knowledge of the research evidence with knowledge of the client's values, cultural beliefs, and life experiences. For example, the research may suggest that a family intervention tends to be the most effective for preventing substance abuse among high-risk adolescents; however, the life experiences of an individual adolescent may lead a practitioner to begin with an alternative treatment approach. Perhaps the teen is afraid to begin a family intervention because the parents have highly conservative views regarding risk behavior. In this case, the practitioner can make a case for family intervention as the best practice, but if it seems as though the youth will refuse any intervention rather than engage in a family intervention, the practitioner may opt for an individual or peer-group intervention that also has some research support.

FUNCTIONS OF RESEARCH FOR EVIDENCE-BASED PRACTICE

For the purposes of this volume, *research* is defined as the systematic application of empirical methods in social work practice for describing worker interventions in scientific terminology. This all-encompassing definition includes interventions applied to individuals, groups, communities, organizations, and societies as a whole. Although few would argue the worthiness of this goal, the functions research should serve in social work practice must be put into proper perspective. The global assumption is that research will be the salvation of social work practice only if more of it is done and done well. The thesis of this volume is that certain ideas pertaining to research are dysfunctional and go beyond the scope of what is worthy of the investment. For example, the question of whether social work is effective, which has occupied the time of many researchers and practitioners for the past four decades, cannot be properly determined through evaluative research (Dean & Reinherz, 1986; Kazdin, 1981; Proctor, 1990; Wodarski, 1981). The question is too general; it is not formulated in terms that are observable and measureable, and, thus, the question is as inappropriate as asking whether the social work profession is relevant to society. The complex question for the evaluation of social work practice consists of six components: client characteristics, worker characteristics, intervention strategies, contextual variables, treatment duration, and relapse-prevention procedures. The guiding questions for evidence-based practitioners are whether these variables lead to positive, sustainable change for clients and how they contribute to change.

Historically, the social worker wants to provide a reason for service that has been questioned; thus, the focus is on applying the technology of research to the evaluation of social work services. However, in order for evaluative research to assess social work services and help provide them on a more rational basis, the global question of whether social work practice is effective has to be restated. Thus, is casework effective utilizing X, Y, and Z techniques in X, Y, and Z contexts with X, Y, and Z therapists and X, Y, and Z clients? For example, clinical research could yield the following proposition: A middle-aged, married, middle-class male with symptoms of depression who has a good work history, a college education, and two children is most effectively treated through brief therapy consisting of structure, ventilation, and clarification in a series of eight sessions provided by a middle-aged, male clinician with a master of social work degree and at least 5 years of clinical practice experience.

Thus, several crucial considerations must be dealt with before research can reasonably be expected to aid the planning and decision-making functions of practitioners, agencies, and institutions involved in the delivery of social services.

PLAUSIBLE STUDIES

Well-designed studies in social work practice specify concretely the unit of change: for example, a client, a group, a community, or an organization. In evaluating social work practice, the unit of change is the individual, group, or system that will be participating in an intervention. Empirically grounded terms also specify how change will occur on some definable continuum. For example, the goal of increasing a client's social functioning would be defined in measurable behavioral objectives—that is, securing and maintaining employment. Likewise, the investigator would also specify how social functioning will be improved: the interventions in which the client will participate. At the same time, a study should specify in what context these interventions will occur and the organizational characteristics of the context, such as agency size, number, and variety of services provided; fluidity of the agency's internal structure; its immediate social environment, administrative style, and supervisors; and so forth. Moreover, the characteristics of the change agent, or the practitioner who will facilitate the intervention, should be clearly stated. For example, the *unit of change* may be ten children between the ages of 11 and 12 in a recreational group at a community center who engage in hitting one another; damaging physical property; running away; climbing out windows; making loud noises; using aggressive verbal statements; and throwing objects, such as paper, candy, erasers, and chairs. The *intervention* in this example is the group worker's use of positive reinforcement to increase prosocial behavior and other behavior modification techniques, such as time-out, shaping, and group contingencies. The *context* in which the intervention is implemented is a community center that offers primarily recreational, leisure time, and educational services for 16,000 enrolled members. Each year, the professional staff of the agency organizes about 200 clubs and classes for children and youths ranging in age from 6 to 18 years. The *change agent* is a female practitioner enrolled in an undergraduate social work program. As the change agent, she is the practitioner who implements the positive reinforcement strategies as an intervention that aims to replace the children's aggressive behaviors with prosocial behaviors.

A well-designed study measures process, or the interventions and services provided, and client outcomes through the duration of the study. The process would allow a better estimate of how the worker's interventions affect the client's behavior. Moreover, through repeated measures of client and worker behavior, the research practitioner can monitor change at small regular intervals (daily or weekly) and, thus, can acquire a more accurate estimate of the effects of worker interventions on client behavior (Bloom et al., 2009).

A significant past error in social work practice was to focus solely on what was to be changed in the client and to proceed only to measure it (Kazdin, 1994). Very seldom did we measure the interventions employed. For example, an evaluation may aim to examine the effectiveness of a behavioral group intervention for children. In implementing this intervention, group workers may use some combination of the following strategies: praise, directions, positive attention, criticism, positive physical contacts, and time-out. Group workers may vary in the types of strategies they use. If the evaluation does not measure which of these strategies are used by various workers, how often they are used, and under what conditions, there is little information about how the intervention is implemented. Therefore, when an evaluation demonstrates that client outcomes have improved, the practitioner has no way of knowing which intervention strategies, worker characteristics, or other factors contributed to the improved outcomes.

WHAT SHOULD BE CHANGED AND WHY

It is essential to understand that the determination of what should be changed involves constant value judgments or a series of them. This is obviously a complex and frequently difficult issue but one that must be considered if services are to be provided on a rational basis. The practitioner immediately confronts the profession's code of ethics as a major determinant in what should be changed, but a code of ethics can serve only as a guide. The answer to what should be changed is not found in quantitative methods of research design technology but, rather, must be dealt with by a complex set of values and norms held by the worker, the client, the agency, and society. The worker's decisions about the target for change must be guided by the research evidence, the client's values and preferences, and his or her own professional judgment about interventions that are a good fit for the client's needs and the context in which services are delivered (Gambrill, 2006). If this issue is not adequately dealt with, it is highly probable that the remainder of the research either will be fruitless or will answer an inappropriate or trivial question.

Most theoretical frameworks in social work show that change is usually defined by the normative structure of the society, whether the changes are in the client, a group of clients, a community, or an organization, such as a social service agency. For example, role theory constructs are used to explain why clients are not performing well in roles as defined by society, and techniques are derived from role theory to modify clients' behavior so they assume their proper societal role. For instance, when young people do not adhere to the traditional values of society, their behaviors are often labeled as dysfunctional, and specific socialization mechanisms are posited to correct these performances (Bennett & Westera, 1994; Hindin, 2007; Jacobs, Rettig, & Bovasso, 1991). A potential deficiency of this approach lies in the tendency to accept the roles formulated by society as given, rather than allowing room to question these roles using a client-centered approach.

If one examines the goals of programs for the poor, delinquent, mentally ill, or developmentally disabled, it is evident that the focus has always been toward the attainment of middle-class values and is evaluated by middle-class criteria, such as having a "good" job, being married, having a "good" income, exhibiting proper social behaviors in particular contexts, and attaining more education. These values continue to be underscored in policies that determine access to public assistance, for example (Thyer & Wodarski, 2007). Relying on these values in implementing social service programs is inconsistent with evidence-based practice, which relies on knowledge of research-supported interventions and cultural competence in making practice decisions. An evidence-based practice approach discourages the continued use of practices that fail to be grounded in client values, because clinicians must integrate knowledge of intervention research with their knowledge of their clients' values.

The majority of research executed in social work and related disciplines has continued to define the outcome criteria in such a way that the research starts with the assumption that an individual must be changed, not his or her social system (Harrison, Wodarski, & Thyer, 1992). Research studies that have well-grounded, empirically defined criteria are needed when the service being evaluated is focused on the individual. However, studies focusing on adequately defined social system variables that may need to be changed to achieve the objectives of a program are also necessary (Wodarski, Feit, Ramey, & Mann, 1995). For example, research indicates that school climate is associated with academic outcomes. Yet, most school-based interventions focus on changing the behavior of individual students or groups of students. Improving student outcomes will, ultimately, require interventions that create a more positive climate in addition to helping students develop new skills (Hopson & Lawson, 2011). Likewise, the rehabilitation of correctional offenders may involve not only programs to change the offender's behaviors but also programs that change society's attitudes or provide decent jobs and housing. Research that focuses on the reciprocal quality of individual and environmental variables will begin to capture the interdependent factors of complex behavior and will lead to the development of empirical theories of human behavior.

Thus, it is the contention of this book that the single most important consideration in the planning and design of practice research is the development, with adequate empirical assessment, of a clear and definitive statement concerning what should be changed. If this issue is not adequately dealt with, undesirable consequences may result, such as insensitivity to clients' needs and values, ineffective intervention efforts, misguided use of personnel and facilities, failure to acquire needed information for planning, and inappropriate change in theory and practice. Yet in many research investigations, this issue is often wholly ignored or given only cursory attention.

THE INTERVENTION APPROACH AND THE CHANGE AGENT

Once a practice problem has been defined and a decision is made concerning what should be changed, the question arises as to what will bring about the desired change. Accomplishing this will require that studies provide detailed information about the processes or interventions that are implemented, in addition to detailed information about outcomes. Although this information has been largely neglected in the past, many interventions now have empirically validated treatment manuals that contain step-by-step procedures, including social skills, relaxation therapy, problem-solving skills, systematic desensitization, and parenting skills (Wodarski, 2009; Wodarski, Rapp-Paglicci, Dulmus, & Jongsma, 2001). Moreover, these manuals facilitate the training of practitioners through exact specifications of directions. The question of which specific operations accounted for the change in these and other practice research studies remains. Even though certain globally defined services were better than others, the exact nature or processes responsible for their success remain unknown. In this age of increasing costs in the delivery of social services, however, it seems to be an ethical obligation to find the most effective components of any seemingly efficacious method of change (Wodarski, Smokowski, & Feit, 1996). Likewise, social workers have a professional and ethical responsibility to use practices that have proven to be effective in helping clients achieve their goals (Gambrill, 2006; National Association of Social Workers, 2008; Wakefield & Kirk, 1996). Thus, research investigations should help isolate those programs and program components that will help clients increase their level of functioning and answer such critical questions as, What is adequate treatment? (i.e., what are the critical components?) Where should it be provided? What qualities should the change agent possess? How long should treatment be provided? What happens if there is no change in the client? Are relapse-prevention procedures necessary?

Research examining the effectiveness of interventions is guided by hypotheses, or predictions about the relationship between independent and dependent variables. Independent variables are predicted to exert some influence on the dependent variables. In social work intervention research, the independent variables are typically the services or interventions provided by the worker, and the dependent variables are the outcomes. It may be that independent variables are too globally conceptualized to be relevant to clients or to be evaluated by research methods. For example, if an evaluation is examining the effectiveness of casework services without defining the services more specifically, the findings will fail to inform social work practitioners about the characteristics of effective casework services. Similarly, if clients participating in one group within an agency demonstrate improved outcomes while clients in another group within the same agency do not, it will be important to measure the strategies used within each group to determine why one group is more effective. If there are no measures of the strategies implemented in each group, the strategies responsible for the change (i.e., structuring group contingencies, use of material reinforcers, use of praise, punishment, extinction, time-out, or shaping) would remain a mystery.

Replication is another important concern and is the cornerstone of training and research. It is difficult to replicate an experiment if the worker cannot precisely specify the nature and magnitude of the intervention; that is a principal reason for the ambiguous outcomes that occur upon replication of an experiment. Similarly, if the precise nature and magnitude of the intervention remains ambiguous, the research does not contribute to building a practice science, even though a positive outcome may be achieved. In other words, if researchers demonstrate that treatment-intervention is successful but they cannot point to the elements of treatment known to be responsible for the positive outcomes, they are not able to teach others how to improve their treatment skills on the basis of their research findings (Kazdin, 2002; Wodarski & Hilarski, in press). Moreover, clients have a right to the least restrictive and least costly methods, as do taxpayers.

All the above points are evidence of a major weakness frequently observed in evaluative research—a general failure to conduct adequate definition and measurement of the independent variable. Many researchers make careful plans and heavy investments in defining and measuring one or more dependent variables and, by comparison, ignore the independent variable altogether. This problem deserves elaboration. For example, a worker conducts an experiment to test the hypothesis—a prediction about the relationship between the independent and dependent variables—that professional casework services will effectively reduce the number of pregnancies among a group of adolescent girls in a vocational high school. To test this hypothesis, girls are randomly assigned to either a control group or an experimental group because random assignment is one of the best known means for holding all other extraneous effects constant. Girls in the control group receive no services, while girls in the experimental group receive casework services. In this example, the term *professional casework* is not an appropriately specified independent variable but is merely a vehicle through which the independent variable will be administered. For professional casework, the terms *solution-focused therapy, problem-solving skills*, the *strengths perspective, behavioral modification*, or *medical treatment* could be substituted, and the same assertion would hold. All these are treatment modalities but tell us little about the specific strategies implemented with clients.

This example represents a case that cannot be adequately dealt with even after specifying the intervention approach or independent variable that will reduce the number of teen pregnancies. Not even the dependent variable has been adequately specified. In order to reduce teen pregnancies, should the professional casework service be directed toward promoting abstinence or use of contraception? Either choice would likely imply a different set of treatments.

In short, there are two means of reducing teen pregnancies: reducing or eliminating sexual activity or promoting the use of contraception. Regardless of the professional treatment modality, researchers must specify the independent variable. In this example, some of the variables that might be considered are training in birth-control techniques, relationships skills, communication skills, problem-solving skills, and cognitive behavioral strategies.

Much of this discussion pertains to issues relating to proper specification of the independent and dependent variables and value judgments concerning what should be changed. Once these have been dealt with, the researcher is in a much better position to select an intervention, but the choice is not then guaranteed. The crucial issue at this point is to decide, using theory and prior knowledge, which interventions can be expected to bring about the desired change. Using, for example, the problem of teen pregnancies, what is there about "casework" that can reasonably reduce teen pregnancies? The proper answer to such a question must be that no one knows. On the other hand, it might reasonably be claimed, based on prior knowledge, that training in contraception will reduce the frequency of pregnancy. No doubt, qualified caseworkers may be selected to provide this training and assist couples or single individuals in getting medical examinations, treatment, prescriptions, and medical supervision. Not all caseworkers are qualified to give such training, and practitioners should be measured or tested to determine that they have the knowledge base necessary for successful administration of the intervention method—in this case, training in use of contraceptives (Wodarski & Wodarski, 1995).

An effective intervention method cannot be specified in global, general terms. It must be specific and directly related to the problem. However, the necessary specificity of the intervention cannot be achieved until the practitioner has dealt explicitly with the evaluative issue of what should be changed and, on that basis, has specified the proper dependent variable in measurable terms. After all that is done, the worker must be certain that the intervention has been so defined and measured as to assure that the intended treatment will be successfully administered. If the worker decides that contraceptive training is the appropriate treatment, the chance of failed treatment and an erroneous research conclusion is possible unless the worker has adequate knowledge to conduct the training.

CRITERIA FOR POSITIVE ASSESSMENT: THE AMOUNT OF CHANGE

In many research studies, the traditional means of judging the adequacy of social work treatment was to compare an experimental group with a control group, or no-treatment group. A treatment is often deemed successful if the client outcomes improve, as predicted, and the changes are statistically significant. Statistical significance means that the changes observed are not likely to occur by chance. This difference from the control or no-treatment group must be considered a necessary outcome before it can be concluded that treatment has produced a "better" or positive outcome. However, the criterion by itself is neither sufficient nor adequate. Improvements among clients in an experimental group may be significantly greater than improvements among clients in a control group. Yet, the participants may not feel that the improvements have a meaningful impact on their lives. For example, Hopson and Holleran Steiker (2010) found that students receiving a substance abuse prevention program reported significant reductions in alcohol use compared with students who did not receive the prevention program. However, focus group discussions with students revealed that they did not perceive a meaningful change in their alcohol use.

Thus, the important question is, does a statistical difference on the measure employed really mean something to the client? In other words, how relevant, important, and meaningful are the criteria for change to the client? For example, many clinical research endeavors have used self-inventories as a basis for evaluating client change. Self-inventories by themselves may be inadequate criteria. For instance, in a well-designed program to change the attitudes of welfare clients toward their work, their attitudes may change but their work habits may remain the same. Likewise, children who are antisocial may perceive significant amounts of change after being involved in treatment even though their behaviors may remain relatively the same. Additionally, traditional designs and statistical techniques that examine changes in groups of individuals do not enable the researcher to assess which individual clients have changed significantly. The objective in social work practice is, often, not to change group scores but to change the behavior of individuals. Here again, the question is posed: what amount of change is necessary to be truly relevant to meeting client needs? In many instances, a statistically significant finding may not lead to the improvement of the client's life.

Statistical significance is an important criterion, for it is used to rule out the hypothesis that research findings could be attributed to chance. However, it tells us virtually nothing about whether the observed change is important. Moreover, the social scientist can nearly always ensure statistically significant outcomes merely by sufficiently increasing the size of the sample. Thus, it is claimed that statistical significance is not a proper criterion for assessing a positive outcome in clinical research. It is necessary but inadequate. Only after achieving statistically significant results can the researcher properly ask, "Was the treatment effective?" When researchers demonstrate statistically significant results, they have effectively ruled out chance (within certain error limits) as one hypothesis to account for the observed outcome, but they have not shown the treatment was effective.

What, then, is meant by "effective" in the context of practice research? That is precisely the issue that must be decided in advance of conducting the study, or at least before the results are in. An experiment, for example, might be conducted to determine whether supportive therapy, positive reinforcement, punishment and deprivation, or intensive psychoanalysis is the preferred modality for improving the performance of underachieving children in a school system. How can positive outcome be judged in these cases? As we have said before, it is not sufficient to show that a statistically significant result was obtained. Suppose, for the sake of argument, that two of the treatments were statistically significant when compared with a control group. That finding, as stated earlier, merely shows that chance is unlikely to account for the observed gains. But how large are the gains? One of the significant treatments may have produced only a 2% gain, while the other produced a 4% gain in performance on relevant criterion variables. One treatment is twice as effective as the other. But how important is a 4% gain? Unfortunately, that is the kind of question that simply cannot be answered by statistical and scientific methods—it involves a value judgment. (This does not mean that value judgments cannot be treated scientifically; they can.) The researchers, the sponsors of the research, the users of the research, and the clients themselves may all have to decide how large a significant (real) observed gain must be before a treatment can be effective. Should an overall gain of specified score points be required, or should the mean score of the target group exceed a specified cutting point, or should every member of the target group obtain a score that exceeds a specified cutting point? A treatment or treatments in clinical research must be judged effective or not by well-defined and specific criteria set at the beginning rather than the end of the research. This is not an easy task; the investigator must determine how much of an effect must be achieved, using a set of explicit values. It can be extremely difficult to disclose the underlying real values that motivate a research study. For example, 2 successes out of 10 in child abuse may be reasonable to justify continuing intervention services. However, such success rates may not be statistically significant. Success in social work needs to be reexamined and set at realistic levels (Howing, Wodarski, Kurtz, & Gaudin, 1993).

A solution to the overreliance on statistical significance is to apply critical thinking in using multiple criteria to evaluate the impact of a social treatment. The treatment effect should be interpreted by how the client perceives the change and various other criteria. Multiple criteria evaluation allows for the measurement of multidimensional behavior. For example, in evaluating a treatment program for antisocial children, a number of criteria could be employed. Various inventories designed to measure antisocial behavior could be completed by children, parents, group therapists, and other significant adults, such as teachers or ministers. Additionally, the attainment of behavioral observational data enables comparisons between perceived behavioral change and actual behavior. Likewise, the subjective evaluation of the interventions by clients, practitioners, and significant others through interviews should be used to assess the practical importance of the intervention. Thus, securing data from various sources allows for a more accurate evaluation of the study outcomes.

Another issue in assessing positive outcome centers on different outcome sources that will be used for evaluation of treatment effects. At the end of treatment, the client may be dissatisfied with the outcome, but the worker may feel that considerable and important changes have been made. How are such potential conflicts to be managed or dealt with? More often than not, these conflicts arise when the goals of the researcher, worker, or agency are being served rather than the goals of the client.

Obviously, the cost of the various treatments must also be weighed when deciding which ones are effective—that is, which produced the largest gain and the least cost. Rarely is the treatment that meets or exceeds the established change criteria also the least expensive in dollar costs or duration, and rarely is the treatment that produces the largest gain at the cheapest cost the treatment of choice. Oftentimes, the problem of competing objectives must be faced: saving money or helping the client. In many cases, one objective can be achieved only at the expense of the other. For example, a treatment may help the client considerably, but the cost of providing it makes it unsustainable. On the other hand, the agency might survive indefinitely if treatment expenditures are not allowed to rise above a specified level, but the treatment that can be given at such costs may be ineffective according to the established change criteria. This is referred to as the minimax principle: minimize losses and maximize gains. However, this is only a principle, and even if it is achievable, it may not be adequate. Five different treatments, for example, may produce statistically significant results and may vary in cost and duration.

The above examples show that selection of the criteria to be used in assessing the outcomes of evaluative research cannot be isolated from the issues previously discussed: what should be changed, what is the properly defined and measured dependent variable, and what is the properly defined and measured independent variable? However, the criteria against which an evaluative study is to be assessed are, more often than not, multiple and require value judgments that rarely, if ever, can be dealt with by using the tools of science. If the practice values concerning what should be changed and the values undergirding the criteria for determining which treatments are effective are not dealt with, it is unlikely that research technology will be of any significance in developing a practice science. Thus, the practitioner will rely heavily on critical thinking and professional expertise to integrate many different sources of information in deciding how to proceed with a client (Gambrill, 2006).

THE EVIDENCE-BASED PRACTITIONER

The evidence-based practitioner in social work views evaluation as an essential ingredient for effective practice. Each intervention technique is offered as a tentative hypothesis awaiting verification. The concepts used to explain and predict the behavior of the client and the worker are always described in observable concrete terms so that communication is clear, open, and concise, not only between the worker and the client but also between the worker and the other professionals who may be working concurrently with the client (Fischer & Corcoran, 2007).

In order to document the effectiveness of a treatment approach, the behaviors of the social worker and the client must always have observable referents; any behavior must be described in such a manner that two or more persons can observe the behavior and agree that it has occurred. These data allow the worker to determine what effect the treatment attempts have produced. This provides the worker with the feedback necessary to assess whether a specific intervention should be continued, discontinued, or revised. Through such an approach, evaluation becomes a central aspect of social work process and a means for practitioners to contribute to the knowledge necessary for effective practice.

These behaviors become even more essential, considering that some social work practice theories have a relatively small body of research supporting their effectiveness. For the evidence-based practitioner, practice theories are ideally chosen from empirical data that support their use. Such an approach to understanding human behavior begins with research that examines formulations about the possible causes of behavior. As research progresses, empirically derived laws are developed according to the existing database. The next step in this process is to disseminate research-based interventions into community settings that serve social work clients (Franklin & Hopson, 2007).

Such a sequential process in theory development and testing, which characterizes applied social psychology and behavioral practice, differs from the manner in which many practice theories that social workers employ were developed. Early theories began with global descriptions of human behavior without experimental data to support their postulates about human behavior. Although these theories do not lack descriptive richness and explanatory potency, they fail to offer highly specific and individualized treatment techniques, and their ability to reliably predict the future behavior of individuals remains to be demonstrated empirically.

Evidence-based practice is critically important under these conditions, when the existing research base is small or nonexistent, because it is the only way to demonstrate that social work interventions are effective, from both the perspective of the worker and the client. It also means that evidence-based practice is part of our ethical responsibility in providing clients with the most effective interventions relevant to their needs.

COMPETENCIES OF THE EVIDENCE-BASED PRACTITIONER

It is necessary to specify objectives for training evidence-based practitioners if social work is to produce personnel capable of evaluating new services to clients; planning, designing, and evaluating adequate service delivery systems; systematically delineating targets for intervention; rigorously assessing methods of change; and, finally, understanding the burgeoning research base of social work and facilitating the dissemination of such knowledge.

The evidence-based practitioner's repertoire of intervention skills involves the systematic application of practice techniques derived from behavioral science theory and supported by empirical evidence to achieve behavior change in clients. The evidence-based practitioner must possess theoretical knowledge and empirical perspective regarding the nature of human behavior, the principles that influence behavioral change, and the empirical data that provide the rationale for the interventions (Dulmus & Wodarski, 1996). The worker also must be capable of translating this knowledge into concrete operations for practical use in different practice settings. In order to be an effective practitioner, therefore, the social worker must possess a solid behavioral science knowledge base and a variety of research skills. Moreover, a thorough grounding in research methodology enables the worker to evaluate therapeutic interventions, a necessary requisite of scientific practice. Because the rigorous training of social workers with scientific perspective equips them to assess and evaluate any instituted practice procedure, this continual evaluation provides corrective feedback to practitioners. For the empirical social worker, theory, practice, and evaluation are all part of one intervention process. The arbitrary division between practice and research, which does not facilitate therapeutic effectiveness or improve practice procedures, is eliminated.

Knowledge Base

The central emphasis is on employing evidence-supported procedures aimed at the solution of the client's difficulties. The body of knowledge the practitioner must possess to be an effective change agent includes the following:

1. A thorough understanding of the scientifically derived theories of behavioral science as they relate to human behavior, personality formation, the development and maintenance of interpersonal relationships, behavior change, and practice intervention

2. The ability to translate behavioral science knowledge into practice technology

3. The skills necessary to assess a study in terms of its methodology and the implications it has for social work practice

4. The ability to objectively evaluate any practice procedure and outcome and formulate new practice strategies when those that originally had been formulated have proven ineffective

5. A working knowledge of a wide variety of research designs, experimental approaches, and statistical procedures, and the ability to use them appropriately for the critical evaluation of one's interventions, whether they take place on the micro or macro levels of society

6. The knowledge of relapse-prevention procedures

Although clients are given the knowledge and tools with which to modify their own behavior, practitioners still take full responsibility in the helping process because their contractual obligations require that they assist the client to modify those specific problems for which professional assistance originally was sought. The social workers' knowledge of the principles of human development and behavior change and their training in practice evaluation enable them to objectively evaluate the outcomes of any intervention program they have devised for a particular client. If a program has been proven ineffective in alleviating a client's distress, the social worker is ethically bound to investigate the reasons for its failure and develop other means of altering the behavior based on evidence.

Overview

The scientific approach to social work practice offers much promise for the social work profession. Based on empirical data and scientific findings, it makes available concrete tools for effective intervention and, most important, builds into the intervention process a problem-solving and evaluative component needed in social work.

Questions for Discussion

1. Explain the role of critical thinking in evidence-based practice.

2. What is the client's role in working with an evidence-based practitioner?

3. How does evidence-based practice relate to the National Association of Social Workers code of ethics?

4. Describe the steps in evidence-based practice.

Evidence-Based Practice Web Resources

SAMHSA's National Registry of Evidence-based Programs and Practices

http://www.nrepp.samhsa.gov/

Office of Juvenile Justice and Delinquency Prevention Model Programs Guide

http://www.ojjdp.gov/mpg/

The Campbell Collaboration

http://www.campbellcollaboration.org/

The Cochrane Collaboration

http://www.cochrane.org/

References

Bennett, L., & Westera, D. (1994). The primacy of relationships for teens: Issues and responses. *Family and Community Health, 17*, 60–69.

Bloom, M., Fischer, J., & Orme, J. G. (2009). *Evaluating practice: Guidelines for the accountable professional* (6th ed.). Boston: Pearson.

Custer, G. (1994, November). Can universities be liable for incompetent grads? *APA Monitor, 25*(11), 7.

Dean, R. G., & Reinherz, H. (1986). Psychodynamic practice and single-system design: The odd couple. *Journal of Social Work Education, 22*(2), 71–81.

Dulmus, C. N., & Wodarski, J. S. (1996). Assessment and effective treatments of childhood psychopathology: Responsibilities and implications for practice. *Journal of Child and Adolescent Group Therapy, 6*(2), 75–99.

Fischer, J., & Corcoran, K. (2007). *Measures for clinical practice: A sourcebook.* New York: Oxford University Press.

Franklin, C., & Hopson, L. (2007). New challenges in research: Translating community-based practices into evidence-based practices. *Journal of Social Work Education, 43*(3), 377–404.

Gambrill, E. (2003). Evidence-based practice: Sea change or emperor's new clothes. *Journal of Social Work Education, 39*(1), 3–23.

Gambrill, E. (2006). Evidence-based practice and policy: Choices ahead. *Research on Social Work Practice, 16,* 338–357.

Harrison, D. F., Wodarski, J. S., & Thyer, B. A. (1992). *Cultural diversity and social work practice.* Springfield, IL: Charles C Thomas.

Hepler, J. B., & Noble, J. H. (1990). Improving social work education: Taking responsibility at the door. *Social Work, 3,* 126–132.

Hindin, M. J. (2007). Role theory. In G. Ritzer (Ed.), *The Blackwell encyclopedia of sociology* (pp. 3959–3962). Hoboken, NJ: Wiley-Blackwell.

Hopson, L., & Holleran Steiker, L. K. (2010). The effectiveness of adaptations of an evidence-based substance abuse prevention program with alternative school students. *Children and Schools, 32*(2), 81–92.

Hopson, L., & Lawson, H. (2011). Social workers' leadership for positive school climates via data-informed planning and decision making. *Children and Schools, 33*(2), 106–118.

Howard, M., Himle, J., Jenson, J., & Vaughn, M. (2009). Revisioning social work clinical education: Recent developments in relation to evidence-based practice. *Journal of Evidence-Based Social Work, 6*(3), 256–273.

Howing, P. T., Wodarski, J. S., Kurtz, D., & Gaudin, J. M. (1993). *Maltreatment and the school-aged child: Developmental outcomes and system issues.* New York: Haworth.

Jacobs, J., Rettig, S., & Bovasso, G. (1991). Change in moral values over three decades, 1958–1988. *Youth and Society, 22,* 468–481.

Kazdin, A. E. (1981). Drawing valid inferences from case studies. *Journal of Consulting and Clinical Psychology, 49,* 183–192.

Kazdin, A. E. (1994). Methodology, design, and evaluation in psychotherapy research. In A. E. Bergin & S. L. Garfield (Eds.), *Handbook of psychotherapy and behavior change* (4th ed.). New York: Wiley.

Kazdin, A. E. (2002). *Research design in clinical psychology* (4th ed.). Columbus, OH: Allyn & Bacon.

Long, K. J., Homesley, L., & Wodarski, J. S. (2007). The role for social workers in the managed health care system: A model for evidence-based practice. In B. A. Thyer & J. S. Wodarski (Eds.), *Social work in mental health: An evidence-based approach.* Hoboken, NJ: Wiley.

Mullen, E., Bledsoe, S., & Bellamy, J. (2008). Implementing evidence-based social work practice. *Research on Social Work Practice, 18*(4), 325–338.

National Association of Social Workers. (2008). *Code of ethics.* Washington, DC: Author.

Proctor, E. (1990). Evaluating clinical practice: Issues of purpose and design. *Social Work Research and Abstracts, 26,* 32–40.

Sackett, D. L., Straus, S. E., Richardson, W. C., Rosenberg, W., & Haynes, R. M. (2000). *Evidence-based medicine: How to practice and teach EBM* (2nd ed.). New York: Churchill Livingstone.

Thyer, B. A. (1995). Effective psychosocial treatments for children: A selected review. *Early Child Development and Care, 106,* 137–147.

Thyer, B. A., & Wodarski, J. S. (Eds.). (2007). *Social work in mental health: An evidence-based approach.* Hoboken, NJ: Wiley.

Wakefield, J., & Kirk, S. (1996). Unscientific thinking about scientific practice: Evaluating the scientist-practitioner model. *Social Work Research, 20,* 83–95.

Wodarski, J. S. (1981). Role of research in clinical practice. Baltimore, MD: University Park Press.

Wodarski, J. S. (2009). *Behavioral medicine: A practitioner's guide.* New York: Haworth.

Wodarski, J. S., Feit, M. D., Ramey, J. H., & Mann, A. (1995). *Social group work in the 21st century.* New York: Haworth.

Wodarski, J. S., & Hilarski, C. (in press). *Handbook of evidence-based social work education.* New York: Haworth.

Wodarski, J. S., Rapp-Paglicci, L. A., Dulmus, C. N., & Jongsma, A. E. (2001). *The social work and human services treatment planner.* New York: Wiley.

Wodarski, J. S., Smokowski, P. R., & Feit, M. D. (1996). Adolescent preventive health: A cost-beneficial social and life group paradigm. *Journal of Prevention and Intervention in the Community, 14*(1/2), 1–40.

Wodarski, L. A., & Wodarski, J. S. (1995). *Adolescent sexuality: A peer/family curriculum.* Springfield, IL: Charles C Thomas.

Criteria for Choosing Knowledge and Assessing Evidence-Based Intervention

Two of the steps in conducting evidence-based practice, as discussed in the previous chapter, are (1) finding the best available evidence relevant for practice decisions and (2) applying critical thinking in analyzing the evidence for its validity, impact on client outcomes, and applicability in practice settings (Gambrill, 2006; Sackett, Straus, Richardson, Rosenberg, & Haynes, 2000). In order to complete these steps successfully, practitioners require the ability to evaluate research studies and translate research into practice generalizations (Briggs & Rzepnicki, 2004; Roberts & Yeager, 2004). This chapter reviews the criteria that may aid practitioners in the assessment of behavioral science research, the use of scientific and practice criteria that can be used to determine the relevance of a study for social work practice, and the characteristics of effective treatment programs for use in comparative evaluations.

SCIENTIFIC CRITERIA FOR THE EVALUATION OF RESEARCH STUDIES

An essential foundation for evidence-based practice is an understanding of the research literature. Evidence-based practitioners employ critical thinking to assess the quality of the research and its relevance for social work practice. Following initial acquaintance with the research process, which can be accomplished through a basic social work research course, practitioners should begin to review research studies in their chosen areas of specialization and evaluate the quality of studies according to the following criteria:

1. *Testability.* Are the basic premises of the study stated in a manner that allows them to be tested adequately? Are the concepts linked to observable events? If not, the basic premises cannot be tested. Moreover, are the key concepts logically interrelated in a consistent, clear, and explicit manner? What are the basic questions and hypotheses of the

study? Are the independent variables specified? Is the question linked in a logical and consistent manner to relevant literature and concepts contained within a particular conceptual framework?

2. *Internal consistency.* How well integrated are the various procedures composing the study? All procedures must be logically consistent. Are concepts operationalized well, meaning that concepts are stated in such a way that they can be measured and observed. Are experimental treatments validated, samples adequately derived, and data inferences checked? Is the study constructed in such a manner that enables answering of the question?

3. *Subsumptive power.* To what extent does the study draw on the available knowledge in the literature? This is assessed by examining the literature review for timeliness, relevancy, and sufficiency in number of references cited. Are research questions formulated in a manner that will add to the available knowledge of social work practice?

4. *Parsimony.* Are the basic relationships between theoretical concepts stated and tested simply and clearly? Practitioners should ask themselves, "Do I really know what is happening in this study?"

5. *Communicability.* To what extent can the findings of the study be communicated to other professionals without distortion and vagueness? Can another practitioner read the study and derive the same conclusions and practice applications? Are the data clearly and concisely communicated? Science is a cumulative social process; hence, it is essential for communications to be clear.

6. *Stimulation value.* To what extent does the study generate other research? How often is it cited in the literature? This criterion reflects the usefulness of a study in producing incentives for other investigators to develop new insights, generate discoveries, and restructure their research endeavors in more profitable ways. How much stimulus value does this study have for me?

7. *Rival factors.* How easily can the basic findings of the study be accounted for by events other than the posited ones, such as history, maturation, testing, instrumentation, regression, selection, mortality, interaction of selection and maturation, interaction of testing and the experimental variable, reactive arrangements, and multiple experimental variable interference (Bloom, Fischer, & Orme, 2009; Campbell, 1967)? These factors are discussed in Chapter 6.

8. *Procedural clarity.* How explicit is the study regarding agreement among various assumptions, relationships, hypotheses, measurement devices, data collection procedures, data analyses, and conclusions? Generally, how well does the study hold together? How well does the study read?

CRITERIA FOR EVALUATING THE RELEVANCE OF RESEARCH FOR SOCIAL WORK PRACTICE

Social work practice typically involves helping clients increase positive behaviors and cognitions related to their treatment goals and decrease those that impede achieving their goals. Therefore, in addition to assessing the quality of a research study, practitioners assess its relevance for informing practice decisions. The following criteria are relevant in determining whether a study adds to practice knowledge:

1. Does the study develop knowledge that will help explain and predict worker and client behaviors in interactional situations in which services are to be provided? Are client and worker variables that influence the interactional situation, such as gender, age, ethnic background, socioeconomic status, and other relevant social attributes, specified?

2. Does the study lead to knowledge that explains what is involved in forming the relationship? What are the basic features of relationship formulation in terms of body language or verbal expression, for example? Maintenance procedures also must be explained. Are these procedures specified for other practitioners?

3. What are the behaviors involved in the attempt to motivate clients to change, teach new skills, or provide important knowledge? How and when should these behaviors be exhibited by the worker? Are criteria clear as to when the different intervention techniques are to occur: how to proceed, at what pace, how long, and when to terminate?

4. Are treatment techniques related to outcome variables? How valid are the assumptions of the study about explaining and predicting behavior? How accurately measured is the amount of change that took place? Is treatment related to behavioral change?

5. If a study provides relevant practice principles, how useful to workers is the knowledge in terms of the accessibility of the variables involved? Can the variables be identified and manipulated? Is the cost-benefit ratio too great? Does the knowledge violate the values and ethics of the profession?

6. Are procedures for relapse prevention addressed? What procedures are specified to ensure the maintenance and generalization of changed behaviors? Have the change agents created the right conditions within the environment to maintain positive change by, for example, substituting "naturally occurring" reinforcers, training relatives or other individuals in the client's environment, gradually removing or fading the contingencies, varying the conditions of training, using different schedules of reinforcement, and using delayed reinforcement and self-control procedures (Kazdin, 2001)? Such procedures are important components of effective social work interventions (Wodarski, 2009).

CHARACTERISTICS OF EVIDENCE-BASED INTERVENTION STRATEGIES

In addition to the criteria above that help practitioners assess whether a study is methodologically strong and useful for informing practice, a growing body of literature describes the common characteristics that effective practices tend to share. Interventions designated as evidence-based practices often share several core characteristics. By familiarizing themselves with these, practitioners can critically assess interventions described in the literature in terms of their consistency with research on best practices. Schinke, Brounstein, and Gardner (2002) report that common characteristics of research-based interventions include

1. program content on general life skills;

2. opportunities to practice newly learned skills through modeling and practicing behaviors during sessions and between sessions;

3. emphasis on consistent support for behavior change from the family, school, and community;

4. use of materials that are clear and easy to follow, such as written manuals that provide step-by-step guidelines for each session;

5. emphasis on relationship building;

6. emphasis on strengths rather than deficits;

7. materials tailored to the target group, implemented by bicultural facilitators when offering the curriculum to minority youth;

8. implementation consistent with curriculum instructions; and

9. booster sessions to maintain positive changes.

These are merely guidelines for assessing the quality of interventions. Some promising and research-based interventions do not meet all the above criteria. For example, the absence of a treatment manual or formal curriculum does not mean that the intervention is ineffective. Social workers serve many populations for whom there are no well-researched interventions. In this case, practitioners can use the tools discussed later in this volume to evaluate their interventions. The following sections provide guidance in evaluating the information provided in the research literature and its consistency with evidence-based practice standards.

CONCEPTUALIZATION AND OPERATIONALIZATION OF TREATMENT

Appropriate conceptualization and operationalization of treatment interventions are imperative for the development of effective programs. Workers must be able to specify which behaviors to implement for a given treatment strategy. This represents a difficult requirement for many theoretical frameworks. Usually, therapeutic services are described on a global level and are assigned a broad label, such as transactional analysis, behavior modification, or family therapy. However, such labels are valuable only so long as they specify the operations involved in implementing the services. For instance, the global label of behavior modification can be separated into the following distinct behavioral acts: directions, positive contact, praise, positive attention, holding, criticism, threats, punishment, negative attention, time-out, and application of a token economy (Kazdin, 2001; Wodarski & Pedi, 1977). Moreover, essential attributes of the change agent that facilitate the implementation of treatment should be delineated. The use of treatment manuals can increase the integrity of the intervention (Wodarski, Wodarski, & Dulmus, 2003).

Rationale for Service Provided

The rationale for offering a program should be based primarily on empirical grounds. This decision-making process includes considering the fit between the agency and the service provided. Relevant considerations include potential barriers to implementing the program, communication structures necessary for effective implementation, types of measures that can be used to evaluate the service, accountability mechanisms that need to be prepared, and procedures for monitoring execution of the program (Bellamy, Bledsoe, Mullen, Fang, & Manuel, 2008; Carpenter-Aeby, Salloum, & Aeby, 2001; Dagenais, Brière, Gratton, & Dupont, 2009; Reid, 1978).

Duration

What criteria will indicate that clients have improved to the extent that services are no longer necessary? When these criteria are defined at the beginning of treatment, they enable workers to determine whether or not a service is meeting the needs of the client and to identify the particular factors involved in deciding whether a service should be terminated. Defining these criteria in specific, behavioral terms will help clinicians and clients make an informed decision about when to begin termination.

For example, a clinician and client may agree that when the client has completed vocational training and obtained employment, they will begin to terminate treatment. A school social worker working with a student who is repeatedly asked to leave the classroom due to disruptive behavior may decide, with the student, family, and teacher, that treatment will be terminated when the student is able to remain in the classroom every day for 3 weeks.

Adequate Specification of Behaviors and Baselines

An adequate treatment program must take into account the need for reliable specification of target behaviors, or those behaviors that are to be changed. For example, a treatment program to alleviate antisocial behavior might employ behavioral rating scales in which the behaviors are concretely specified. These could include such observable behaviors as hitting others, damaging physical property, running away, climbing and jumping out windows, throwing objects, and making loud noises and aggressive or threatening verbal statements.

A prerequisite for the adequate evaluation of any therapeutic service is securing a baseline before treatment. A baseline measurement provides a record of the state of the presenting problem before an intervention is provided. For example, a practitioner may observe a child in a classroom and record the number of behavioral incidents 2 days per week for 2 weeks prior to beginning an intervention. Subsequent measurement data can be compared with the baseline data to determine whether clients have improved in targeted areas. Referring back to the example, the practitioner could continue to conduct behavioral observations twice per week while providing a behavior intervention with the child. This enables the practitioner to assess how treatment interventions compare with no treatment interventions.

Measures of Therapist and Client Behaviors

Various measures such as checklists filled out by children and significant others (e.g., group leaders, parents, referral agencies, or grandparents) and behavioral time-sampling schedules can be used to assess change in clients (Bloom et al., 2009; Wodarski & Rittner, 1995). Likewise, behavioral rating scales can be used to assess the behaviors exhibited by a change agent. These and other measures are reviewed in Chapter 5.

The literature of the past decade has called for multicriteria measurement processes for the evaluation of therapeutic services. However, investigators who have used multi-criteria measurement indicate that many changes observed with some inventories do not necessarily correspond with results of other inventories used in the same evaluation. For example, studies by Wodarski and colleagues (Wodarski & Buckholdt, 1975; Wodarski, Feldman, & Pedi, 1976; Wodarski & Pedi, 1977, 1978; Wodarski, 2009) found little correlation between self-inventory and behavioral rating scales. In many instances, a change can occur on one of the measurements and not on another measurement. When using multiple measures, it is helpful to include a direct measure of behavior, such as behavioral observation, in addition to indirect measures of behavior, such as self-report inventories (Bloom et al., 2009). It is important to consider the strengths and limitations of any measure used in a study. Because every measurement strategy is likely to have some limitations, using multiple types of measures strengthens a study. If the measures are weak, it is difficult to know whether your data reflect change in client outcomes, or inconsistencies or bias in the measure. Measurement issues will be discussed in greater detail in Chapter 5.

Designs

It frequently has been assumed that the only way therapeutic services can be evaluated is by employing classical experimental designs—those in which participants are assigned randomly to one or more experimental or control groups. However, such designs may not be the most appropriate for the evaluation of services. Implementing these designs may be costly in money, energy, and administration. Moreover, the criterion of random assignment of participants is usually hard to meet in the evaluation of services provided to clients. New time-series designs, however, are emerging from behavior modification literature (see Chapter 7). The designs are easily implemented in social work practice contexts; they cost less money, energy, and administrative execution. These designs provide pilot data that enable a worker to determine if interventions have had an effect on client behaviors.

The emphasis on the use of traditional experimental designs, which involve grouping clients into experimental and control groups, in the evaluation of services in social work is diametrically opposed to a basic practice assumption—namely, that every individual is unique and needs to be considered in his or her own gestalt. The single-case study, which has been championed in recent behavior modification research, may alleviate many of the measurement problems discussed. In this approach, clients serve as their own control, and a client's change is evaluated against data provided during a baseline period that precedes the application of treatment. Chapters 6 and 7 provide criteria by which the worker can determine the appropriateness of the design chosen for evaluation.

Statistics

Evaluation involves several means of assessing whether significant change has taken place. Evaluation of therapeutic services entails the construction of tables and graphs of client and therapist behaviors. Usually, graphs are constructed from measures of central tendencies, such as the mean, mode, or median. A common error in social work practice is to focus solely on what is to be changed in the client and to proceed only to measure that change. Sophisticated evaluation programs measure the behaviors of the client and the change agent simultaneously to enable assessment of how the change agent's behavior has affected the client.

Guidelines on acceptable levels of change are being developed through meta-analysis of numerous studies. Meta-analyses synthesize findings from multiple studies of the same intervention and provide the typical size of the effect of that intervention (Johnson, Scott-Sheldon, & Carey, 2010). These studies typically report an average effect size, a statistic indicating the magnitude of a change in behavior. For example, a meta-analysis of behavioral intervention research would examine the effects of behavioral interventions across a range of studies and provide the average effect size for the intervention. These results can be helpful in determining the typical size of the intervention's effect so that the research can set reasonable expectations for behavior change.

Treatment Monitoring

Having met all prerequisites, it then becomes necessary to monitor the implementation of treatment throughout so that necessary adjustments can be made over time if the quality of treatment varies. If behavioral change is obtained and the investigator can provide data to indicate that treatments were differentially implemented, the change agents can claim with confidence that their treatment is responsible for the observed modifications in behavior. However, if such data cannot be provided when client change has occurred, many rival hypotheses can be postulated to account for the results.

Follow-up

The proper assessment of any therapeutic program with clients involves follow-up. Crucial questions answered by follow-up include whether a therapeutic program has changed behaviors in a desired direction, how long these behaviors were maintained, and to what other contexts they generalized. Has the practitioner worked to maintain positive changes by substituting "naturally occurring" reinforcers, training relatives or other individuals in the client's environment, gradually removing or fading the contingencies, varying the conditions of training, using different schedules of reinforcement, and using delayed reinforcement and self-control procedures (Kazdin, 2001)? Such procedures will be employed in future sophisticated and effective social service delivery systems. Pertinent questions remain concerning when and where a follow-up should occur, how long it should last, and who should secure the measurement. Empirical guidelines for these questions are yet to be developed. Usual procedures include follow-ups 1 and 2 years after service has been provided (Wodarski, 2009).

Overview

This chapter equips practitioners with an overview of the tools used to evaluate studies and assess whether or not the knowledge is relevant to social work practice. A set of criteria are provided that enable the evaluation of treatment programs reported in the literature. As the knowledge produced by the behavioral sciences increases, such criteria will become part of a skill repertoire to aid empirical practitioners in choosing the complex knowledge needed in practice.

Questions for Discussion

1. An article reports that a behavioral intervention resulted in significant improvement in the behavior of a group of fourth-graders with a history of disruptive behavior. What criteria would you use to determine whether you should use these findings to inform your practice as a school social worker?

2. Write a script that you could use to discuss with a client the research on a particular intervention. Practice reading the script aloud. Consider how the information would be received by a client.

3. How would you apply the steps of evidence-based practice if you were working with a client whose presenting problem has not been well researched?

References

Bellamy, J. L., Bledsoe, S. E., Mullen, E. J., Fang, L., & Manuel, J. I. (2008). Agency-university partnership for evidence-based practice in social work. *Journal of Social Work Education, 44*(3), 55–75.

Bloom, M., Fischer, J., & Orme, J. (2009). *Evaluating practice: Guidelines for the accountable professional* (6th ed.). Boston: Allyn & Bacon.

Briggs, H. E., & Rzepnicki, T. L. (Eds.). (2004). *Using evidence in social work practice: Behavioral perspectives.* Chicago: Lyceum.

Campbell, D. T. (1967). From description to experimentation: Interpreting trends as quasi-experiments. In C. W. Harris (Ed.), *Problems in measuring change* (pp. 112–142). Madison: University of Wisconsin Press.

Carpenter-Aeby, T., Salloum, M., & Aeby, V. G. (2001). A process evaluation of school social work services in a disciplinary alternative educational program. *Children and Schools, 23*(3), 171–181.

Dagenais, C., Brière, F. N., Gratton, G., & Dupont, D. (2009). Brief and intensive family support program to prevent emergency placements: Lessons learned from a process evaluation. *Children and Youth Services Review, 31*(5), 594–600.

Gambrill, E. (2006). Evidence-based practice and policy: Choices ahead. *Research on Social Work Practice, 16,* 338–357.

Johnson, B. T., Scott-Sheldon, L. A. J., & Carey, M. P. (2010). Meta-synthesis of health behavior change meta-analyses. *American Journal of Public Health, 100*(11), 2193–2198.

Kazdin, A. E. (2001). *Behavior modification in applied settings* (6th ed.). Homewood, IL: Dorsey.

Reid, W. J. (1978). The social agency as a research machine. *Journal of Social Service Research, 2*(1), 11–23.

Roberts, A. R., & Yeager, K. R. (2004). *Evidence-based practice manual: Research and outcome measures in health and human services.* New York: Oxford University Press.

Sackett, D. L., Straus, S. E., Richardson, W. C, Rosenberg, W., & Haynes, R. M. (2000). *Evidence-based medicine: How to practice and teach EBM* (2nd ed.). New York: Churchill Livingstone.

Schinke, S., Brounstein, P., & Gardner, S. (2002). *Science-based prevention programs and principles, 2002.* Rockville, MD: Substance Abuse and Mental Health Services Administration, Center for Substance Abuse Prevention.

Wodarski, J. S. (2009). *Behavioral medicine: A social worker's guide.* New York: Routledge.

Wodarski, J. S., & Buckholdt, D. (1975). Behavioral instruction in college classrooms: A review of methodological procedures. In J. M. Johnston (Ed.), *Behavior research and technology in higher education.* Springfield, IL: Charles C Thomas.

Wodarski, J. S., Feldman, R. A., & Pedi, S. J. (1976). The comparison of prosocial and antisocial children on multicriterion measures at summer camp: A three-year study. *Social Service Review, 3,* 255–273.

Wodarski, J. S., & Pedi, S. J. (1977). The comparison of antisocial and prosocial children on multicriterion measures at a community center: A three-year study. *Social Work, 22,* 290–296.

Wodarski, J. S., & Pedi, S. J. (1978). The empirical evaluation of the effects of different group-treatment strategies against a controlled treatment strategy on behavior exhibited by antisocial children, behavior of the therapist, and two self-ratings measuring antisocial behavior. *Journal of Clinical Psychology 34,* 471–481.

Wodarski, J. S., & Rittner, B. (1995). Clinical instruments: Assessing and treating children and families. *Early Child Development and Care, 106,* 43–58.

Wodarski, J. S., Wodarski, L. A., & Dulmus, C. N. (2003). *Adolescent depression and suicide: A comprehensive empirical intervention for prevention and treatment.* Springfield, IL: Charles C Thomas.

Transforming Behavioral Science Knowledge Into Evidence-Based Practice Generalizations

The preceding chapter focused on criteria for selecting knowledge from the behavior science for social work practice. This chapter illustrates how knowledge from the social sciences can be utilized to form beginning practice generalizations. More specifically, it illustrates how practitioners can apply research evidence related to worker and client characteristics, intervention approaches, treatment context, duration, and relapse-prevention procedures.

The sheer volume of studies makes the translation of behavioral science knowledge into practice principles a difficult task (Thyer & Wodarski, 2007). This chapter provides an example of how such translations may take place and serves as a prototype for future endeavors, as illustrated by selected and classic studies.

WORKER CHARACTERISTICS

Similarity of Client and Worker

Worker variables, such as socioeconomic status, race and ethnicity, religion, age, gender, and communication skills, have been linked to therapeutic outcomes. One practice generalization taken from the literature is that similarities between clients and workers can improve engagement and outcomes (Long, Homesley, & Wodarski, 2007). For example, a growing body of research demonstrates that matching clients with a clinician from a similar cultural or ethnic background can improve outcomes for Hispanic clients (Field & Caetano, 2010; Flicker, Waidron, Turner, Brody, & Hops, 2008; Halliday-Boykins, Schoenwald, & Letourneau, 2005). Other researchers contend that this cultural or ethnic matching is not essential if clinicians are culturally sensitive and have past experience working with clients from the cultural group they serve (Manoleas, 1994; Perry & Limb, 2004). Less experienced practitioners may have more success engaging and retaining clients in treatment if they work with clients who are similar to themselves on relevant attributes. Support for this proposition also is derived from literature on attraction, which indicates that similarity between workers and clients on certain variables increases the attractiveness of the therapeutic context, thus increasing the probability that clients will remain in therapy, a necessary condition for behavioral change (Fisher & O'Donohue, 2006).

Worker–Client Relationships

The quality of the working relationship between the worker and client is typically referred to as the working alliance or therapeutic alliance. This alliance has demonstrated a modest, but consistent, relationship with outcomes in research conducted on a range of therapeutic practices (Horvath & Bedi, 2002). The Division of Psychotherapy of the American Psychological Association commissioned a task force to examine the characteristics of therapy relationships that are empirically supported as having an effect on client outcomes (Scaturo, 2010). The task force identified the following factors as having solid research support: (1) the therapeutic alliance, (2) empathy, and (3) goal consensus and collaboration. Factors with a less robust but still promising level of research support included (1) positive regard, (2) congruence and genuineness, (3) feedback from the therapist, (4) attention to and repairs of disrupted alliances, (5) appropriate self-disclosure from the therapist, (6) management of countertransference, and (7) the therapist's ability to interpret the relationship for the client (Norcross, 2002; Norcross & Hill, 2004; Scaturo, 2010).

Communications Regarding Expectations for Change and Competence

Workers who communicate positive expectations for change facilitate positive therapeutic outcomes because the clients' expectations are powerful determinants of counseling effectiveness. Clients expect their workers to be experienced, skilled, genuine, accepting, and to exhibit expert and trusting behaviors (Goldfried & Davison, 1994; Rosenthal, 1976; Tinsley & Harris, 1976). Studies indicate that a worker can demonstrate credibility by being organized, providing structure in defining the client's and worker's roles in therapy, suggesting appropriate topics for beginning discussions, and engaging in proper nonverbal communication; the worker can establish trust by being attentive, leaning toward the client, using responsive facial expressions and appropriate head nods, and maintaining an attentive posture (Shealy, 1995; Wodarski, 2009). Clients also report a stronger therapeutic relationship with their worker when the worker offers advice or challenges them through disagreeing, providing alternatives, or requesting explanations.

Positive Communications

Clients and clinicians are more likely to develop a therapeutic alliance when clients sense that the clinician is actively listening to them and processing their statements (Nugent & Halvorson, 1995). The worker can signal that messages have been received through appropriate verbal statements and through nonverbal means, such as proper eye contact. These operations signify to the client that the worker has been listening, a rewarding interaction that should increase the probability of relationship continuance (Horvath & Greenberg, 1989; Seabury, 1980; Weger, Castle, & Emmett, 2010). These component variables are conceptualized as "verbal congruence."

Practice Recommendations

Many researchers have studied worker variables and their relationship to therapeutic outcome; thus, empirical statements can be made regarding worker variables and their influence on practice. Based on the research literature, the following practices are recommended:

1. Matching clients and workers with similar attributes can facilitate development of a therapeutic alliance. This may be especially important for less-experienced workers.

2. Cultural competence is critical for successful engagement with clients, retention in treatment, and achieving positive outcomes for culturally and ethnically diverse clients.

3. The worker's ability to successfully communicate empathy, warmth, and genuineness is essential to creating strong working relationships with clients.

4. Practitioners need both verbal and nonverbal communication skills to engage clients and develop credibility. Practitioners who exhibit credibility and communicate acceptance of the client create the expectation that the therapeutic process will produce desired changes.

Table 3.1 summarizes the common features of an effective worker, based on replicated studies (Shealy, 1995).

TABLE 3.1   Common Factors of Worker Efficacy
Congruency
Acceptance/unconditional positive regard
Empathy
Understanding/communication of understanding
Encourages autonomy, responsibility
Ability to relate/develop alliance
Well-adjusted
Interest in helping
Provides treatment as intended
Exploration of client needs and values
Expectation for improvement
Emotionally stimulating/challenging/not afraid of confrontation
Firm, direct; can set limits
Works hard for client/persistent
Nurturing

CLIENT CHARACTERISTICS

Client characteristics, including age, gender, race and ethnicity, values, attitudes, socioeconomic status, and readiness for change, are associated with practice effectiveness (Thyer, Wodarski, Myers, & Harrison, 2010). In some cases, the research suggests that clients and workers should be matched on some of these attributes in order to promote engagement, encourage a positive working relationship, and improve outcomes (Thyer et al., 2010). The following sections provide an overview of selected research studies aimed at determining the effects of these variables on intervention outcome.

Age

Older adults are underserved by mental health service systems in part because of a reluctance to seek services and also because of a shortage of mental health professionals trained to serve this population (Gellis, McClive, & Brown, 2009). The stigma associated with mental health disorders and difficulty accessing services are significant barriers. Mental health disorders common among older adults include depression and anxiety. Few studies have examined the effect of age on the client–counselor relationship. According to Harrison and Dziegielewski (1992), growing old in general continues to be viewed negatively in our society, not only by those who are younger but also by many healthcare and mental healthcare professionals. These authors view older adults as victims of societal attitudes that devalue old age.

> Many individuals (young and old) will do almost anything to avoid or deny old age. Such prejudices are the result of both rational and irrational fears. Rational fears of declines in health, income, losses of loved ones, and social status can be exaggerated by our negative stereotypes of the elderly and the irrational fears of changes in appearance, loss of masculinity, femininity, and perceived mental incompetence. The elderly continue to be oppressed by myths and misinformation and by real obstacles imposed by various biological, psychological, social and economic factors. (p. 209)

Harrison and Dziegielewski (1992) suggest that social workers, at a minimum, should examine their own attitudes toward aging and older adults. They should not, directly or indirectly, discriminate based on age; this attitude results in ineffective and unethical practice. Practitioners need to recognize the aged as a valuable resource in society and provide services and advocacy that will maximize the older person's degree of life satisfaction and well-being.

Gender

Much of the research on practice effectiveness examines differences in outcomes by gender. While the findings are mixed, they indicate that male and female clients relate to their workers differently. Women involved in couples counseling, for example, are more likely than men to report bonding with their worker (Werner-Wilson, Michaels, Thomas, & Thiesen, 2003). Women also tend to have more positive attitudes about seeking help (Nam et al., 2010). Although the research does not indicate a clear benefit in terms of therapeutic outcomes for matching clients according to gender (Blow, Timm, & Cox, 2008), gender matching promotes remaining in treatment until completion (Wintersteen, Mensinger, & Diamond, 2005).

Evidence also suggests that mental health practitioners generally hold different mental health standards for men and women and see traditional male behavior as more healthy than traditional female behavior (Hampton, Lambert, & Snell, 1986; Kabacoff, Marwit, & Orlofsky, 1985; Kravetz & Jones, 1981; Leventhal & Martell, 2006). Undoubtedly, every currently identified psychological construct has been examined for its differential distribution by gender. Many of these examinations have revealed statistically significant differences. In examining the meta-analytic reviews of this research, however, Deaux (1984) noted that 95% of the variance was explained by factors other than gender differences.

Research also has demonstrated gender differences in the prevalence of various mental health diagnoses (Leland, 1982; Leventhal & Martell, 2006; Myers et al., 1984; Robins et al., 1984; Schaffer, 1981; Travis, 1988; Widom, 1984). Specifically, women are diagnosed with depression and anxiety (including panic disorders, phobias, and obsessive-compulsive disorders) at rates two to three times higher than those of men, while diagnosis rates of alcoholism, drug dependence, and personality disorders are five to six times higher among men. Women attempt suicide at a rate two to three times higher than that of men (Krug, Dahlberg, Mercy, Zwi, & Lozano, 2002). However, men account for 79% of suicides, and the rate of completed suicides among men is four times higher than that among women (Centers for Disease Control and Prevention, 2009). Women are more likely than men to suffer from eating disorders, including obesity (Attie & Brooks-Gunn, 1987; Fisher & O'Donohue, 2006).

Race and Ethnicity

Racial influences on treatment have received renewed attention in the literature, with more than a fourfold increase in studies over the past 20 years. These studies, however, have been mainly descriptive. Problems of small sample size and unreliable measures are prevalent. Many articles are simply reviews of the literature based on theoretical knowledge, with data derived only from nonsystematic recordings of the author's clinical experiences.

Mounting evidence indicates that racial and ethnic minority groups are less likely to access mental health services and are less satisfied with services they receive. Possible reasons for this disparity include the stigma surrounding the receipt of mental health services, concerns about medications, distrust of providers, and a need for improved cultural competence among providers (Kleinman & Benson, 2006; Whitley, 2009).

The data are inconclusive regarding the influence of race and ethnicity on therapeutic outcomes. Some studies suggest that matching clients and workers by race and ethnicity is helpful, but not essential, for achieving positive outcomes. In a study examining the impact of ethnic similarity on therapeutic alliance and outcomes, findings indicate that clients who were ethnically similar to their workers had more positive outcomes than their peers who were not paired with an ethnically similar worker (Ricker, Nystul, & Waldo, 1999). However, ethnic pairings had no relationship with the therapeutic alliance, which was also unrelated to outcomes. Other research suggests that matching workers and clients by race and ethnicity results in better retention in treatment (Wintersteen et al., 2005). Ethnic similarity also may be important for clients who are not acculturated to the dominant culture. These clients are likely to prefer working with someone who shares their values and can speak their native language (Padilla & Perez, 2003; Paris, Bedregal, Añez, Shahar, & Davidson, 2004). Other data suggest that worker competence and knowledge of the client's problems are more important than matching workers and clients by race and ethnicity (Thyer et al., 2010).

Although the research findings in this area illustrate the complexity of the relationship between race and ethnicity and treatment outcomes, the themes that emerge suggest that worker–client similarity may promote engagement in treatment and retention. This theme is also prevalent in the research on cultural adaptations of evidence-based prevention programs. Adapting a program for a particular ethnic group and engaging racially or ethnically similar facilitators may not improve treatment outcomes directly, but it may result in better recruitment and retention (Kumpfer, Alvarado, Smith, & Bellamy, 2002). Clearly, more research is needed to better understand the impact of race and ethnicity on treatment outcomes (Thyer et al., 2010).

Socioeconomic Status

Socioeconomic status is a powerful predictor of outcomes. Poverty is associated with a range of negative outcomes, including dropping out of high school, unemployment, substance abuse, chronic health conditions, and suicide. The stressors associated with economic deprivation are intertwined with the history of oppression and discrimination experienced by many racial and ethnic minority groups since these groups are overrepresented in impoverished neighborhoods (Fraser, Kirby, & Smokowski, 2004).

The effects of poverty are wide reaching. When families experience economic hardship, parents are more likely to experience psychological distress and employ poor family management practices. The stressors associated with economic hardship may cause interparental conflict, which can impair parent–child relationships and result in increased aggressive behavior among children. The disorganization and safety problems associated with impoverished neighborhoods create a stressful environment as well. The high rates of unemployment, crime, violence, mobility, and single-parent families that characterize many impoverished communities create a climate of collective poverty. Inadequate access to high-quality schools, healthcare, positive role models, and employment opportunities creates a neighborhood climate that often encourages engagement in illicit activities and risk behaviors, such as substance abuse (Fraser, Kirby, & Smokowski, 2004). Practitioners also need to be aware of ways social forces associated with poverty and discrimination contribute to the problems experienced by racial and ethnic minority groups (Kropf & Isaac, 1992).

YAVIS Versus Non-YAVIS

Research conducted during the 1960s, 1970s, and 1980s suggested that clinicians are influenced by a bias toward serving the young, attractive, verbal, intelligent, and successful (YAVIS) (Henry, Sims, & Spray, 1971, 1973; Jennings & Davis, 1977; Schofield, 1964). In 1964, William Schofield published a book containing the results of an interesting survey of psychiatrists, psychologists, and social workers who were involved in private practice. Participants were asked to describe their case load with variables descriptive of their "typical" clients and also the characteristics of their "ideal" clients. On the average, more than half of each sample of therapists expressed a distinct preference with respect to the ideal client's age, marital status, and educational and occupational levels.

Although this research was conducted decades ago, some similar themes inform research on the therapeutic alliance today. Some evidence suggests that clients are more likely to rate their workers as supportive and trustworthy when the workers perceive the clients as attractive, active participants and as goal oriented. However, while clients who are perceived as active participants and goal oriented tend to have better outcomes, attractiveness does not seem to be related to outcomes (Ramnerö & Öst, 2007). This research points to the importance of self-awareness on the part of workers to assess whether their perceptions of clients may be influencing delivery of services.

Stages of Change

The transtheoretical model that conceptualizes a client's readiness for change was developed by Prochaska and DiClemente (1982). Their observations led to the notion that people go through similar stages of change, no matter the therapy. The model suggests that different intervention approaches are needed for people at different stages of change and specifies which processes are most important at each stage.

Prochaska (1996) suggests that the stage paradigm involves a six-stage change process.

- Precontemplation: Not intending to take action in the near future. Individuals in this stage are typically defensive and resistant; some are demoralized by past failures.

- Contemplation: Intending to take action in the near future. Individuals are aware of the benefits of change, as well as the cost of change.

- Preparation: Ready to participate in action-oriented interventions. Motivation is most important at this level.

- Action: Involves overt behavior modification.

- Maintenance: Continue to apply processes of change but do not have to work as hard. This is a common time for relapse. Some will remain in this stage for the rest of their lives.

- Termination: Period of no longer having to apply process of change. Some never reach this state.

Understanding a client's readiness for change is critical if workers are to be responsive to their clients and employ interventions that are an appropriate fit for each client. For example, a well-researched intervention to reduce substance abuse is unlikely to be effective if the client has not acknowledged that his or her substance use is a problem and has no intention of changing his or her behavior. Some interventions, such as motivational interviewing, are designed to respond to clients at different stages of change and move them along this continuum to improve their readiness for change (van Wormer, 2007).

Practice Recommendations

The following practice generalizations can be derived from results of studies cited in this section:

1. The worker should be trained to recognize the effects of client characteristics, such as age, race, ethnicity, and socioeconomic status, on therapeutic outcome.

2. If client and worker are significantly different on relevant variables, pretraining can prepare the worker for engaging with clients from different cultural backgrounds or life experiences. The client also should receive preparation on what to expect from the worker. Although the research on the benefits of client–worker similarity yields mixed findings, these similarities may promote engagement in treatment and retention.

3. Attentiveness to a client's readiness for change is critical for choosing appropriate interventions that are likely to succeed in helping the client change his or her behavior.

TREATMENT COMPONENTS

Length of Therapy

In the past four decades, a substantial number of evaluative studies have had a profound impact on traditional therapeutic practice. Major changes have come about as a result of these studies, one in particular being the length of therapy. In the past, therapy was considered to be a long and involved process (Fischer, 1978). Current trends, however, indicate that the optimal number of visits is between 8 and 16. Current research indicates that brief, directive interventions have a consistent outcome advantage in the treatment of a multitude of disorders (Giles, Prial, & Neims, 1993; Schinke, Brounstein, & Gardner, 2002). Moreover, in response to research support for brief treatments, managed health-care will often provide payment only for empirically based treatments of a short duration (Johnstone et al., 1995; Long, Homesley, & Wodarski, 2007; Nicholson, Dine-Young, Simon, Fisher, & Bateman, 1996).

Behavior Acquisition

A second focus involves helping clients learn new behaviors to deal with their specific situations. This emphasis is a departure from the practice of first changing attitudes or motivation and positing that behavior change will follow. Accumulating research evidence indicates that if clients are taught behaviors that enable them to influence their external and internal environments (e.g., self-management procedure, appropriate assertive behavior, and problem solving), their social functioning will increase (Wodarski, 2009).

Development of behaviors is believed to occur optimally in structured therapeutic contexts—that is, where intervention procedures follow a sequential pattern to develop and maintain socially relevant behaviors. Such patterns usually consist of mutually agreed-on contracts that include goals, methods, termination criteria, and the rights and responsibilities of client and worker. Two examples of historically empirically based treatment technologies are task-centered casework and behavioral approaches.

Task-Centered Casework

Task-centered casework is a theoretical system of short-term intervention that emerged in 1972 with the publication of *Task-Centered Casework,* by Reid and Epstein. Reid and Epstein (1977) published a follow-up book, *Task-Centered Practice,* and in another book, *Task-Centered System,* Reid (1978) nicely elucidated the relevant aspects of the task-centered approach. Task-centered casework is unique in development because researchers and practitioners have worked together to specify its constructs and have tested various aspects of the total intervention package.

In 1975, Reid took a major step in placing task-centered casework on firm empirical ground by operationalizing the variable of task performance in a five-step plan called task implementation sequence. The plan is a progressive treatment sequence that includes "enhancing commitment, planning task implementation, analyzing obstacles, modeling, rehearsal, guided practice, and summarizing," with the goal of eliciting specific client behaviors. The introduction of "operational tasks" is part of a beginning effort to specify the model's constructs and, thereby, place the paradigm on firmer scientific ground by specifying the unit of attention—the task—in more measurable terms. Three keys to the success of task-centered casework may be the structural elements of the model, its emphasis on short-term service, and the specification of goals to be achieved by the client in concrete steps (Colvin, Lee, Magnano, & Smith, 2008; Reid, 1997).

Behavioral Approaches

Along with the development of the task-centered approach, corresponding and enhancing treatment technologies have been developed. These consist of behavioral approaches to the solution of interpersonal problems (Wodarski & Hilarski, 2006). Numerous data-based behavioral technologies are available for workers to use in helping clients acquire necessary behaviors to operate in their environments.

The following is a categorization of the areas of possible application of behavioral technology in social work practice. Each application has substantial empirical support. A further elaboration of theory, research, and application of the techniques is available in *Social Work in Mental Health: An Evidence-Based Approach* (Thyer & Wodarski, 2007) and *Behavioral Medicine* (Wodarski, 2009).

Children

1. *Foster care services* involve helping natural and foster parents acquire appropriate parenting skills and develop behavior-management programs. Strategies include helping parents use contingency contracts, stimulus control, and time-out procedures to facilitate their children's development of the social skills needed for effective adult functioning.

2. *Schools* can use behavioral strategies to decrease absenteeism; increase appropriate academic behavior such as reading comprehension, vocabulary development, and computational skills; increase interpersonal skills, such as the ability to share and cooperate with other children and adults; and decrease disruptive behaviors.

3. *Juvenile courts* help decrease deviant behavior and increase prosocial behavior through contingency contracting, programming significant adults to provide reinforcement for prosocial behavior, and developing programs for training children in those behavioral skills that will allow them to experience satisfaction and gain desired reinforcements through socially acceptable means.

4. *Community centers* help children develop appropriate social skills, such as working together, participating in decision making, making plans, and discussing and completing plans successfully.

5. *Outpatient clinics* help clients reduce anxiety, eliminate disturbing behavioral problems, define career and lifestyle goals, increase self-esteem, gain employment, solve problems (both concrete and interpersonal), develop satisfying lifestyles, and learn skills necessary for successful adult functioning in society.

Adults

1. *Family service* helps develop marital interactional skills for effective problem-solving and goal-setting behaviors, development of better parenting behaviors, and development of clearer communication structures to facilitate interaction among family members.

2. *Community health and mental health centers* help individuals reduce anxieties through relaxation techniques; teaching self-control to enable clients to alter certain problem-causing behaviors; offering assertiveness training as one means of meeting personal needs; and helping in the acquisition of behaviors to facilitate interaction with family, friends, and coworkers.

3. *Psychiatric hospitals* use token economies to help clients acquire necessary prosocial behaviors for their effective reintegration into society, structuring clients' environments through provision of reinforcement by significant others for the maintenance of appropriate social behaviors, such as self-care, employment, and social interactional skills.

4. *Public welfare* helps clients achieve self-sufficiency; learn effective child-management and financial-management procedures; and develop social behaviors, skills, and competencies needed to gain employment.

5. *Corrections* use token economies to increase prosocial behaviors, teach new job skills, and help clients develop self-control and prosocial problem-solving strategies

Some technologies with accumulating empirical histories include

- relaxation training,
- assertiveness training,
- anger management,
- stress management,
- problem-solving skills,
- self-esteem building,
- urge control,
- relapse prevention,
- eye movement desensitization and reprocessing, and
- mindfulness-based cognitive therapy.

IMPLEMENTATION OF CHANGE STRATEGY

Social work has been characterized historically as a profession that emphasizes a one-to-one relationship with clients to achieve behavioral change (Glenn & Kunnes, 1973; Levine & Perkins, 1987; Ryan, 1971; Specht & Courtney, 1993; Wodarski, 1994). The profession has seldom adequately addressed the appropriateness of the various service-delivery mechanisms for certain types of clients, however. Few empirical studies have delineated the parameters of criteria for determining whether one-to-one or group-level treatment is best for achieving behavioral change in a given situation.

Individual Treatment Versus Group Treatment

Even though recent years have witnessed a growing emphasis on group treatment for clients as a result of various conceptualizations that place a heavy emphasis on the roles clients' peers and significant others play, relatively few clients are provided with group, as opposed to individual, interventions. Yet, a number of deficiencies are obvious in placement of clients in individual casework services. The casework relationship is unlike most situations faced in daily interaction. In contrast, the provision of services in groups offers the following benefits: The group's interactional situation more frequently typifies many kinds of daily interactions. Services facilitating the development of behaviors that enable people to interact in groups are likely to better prepare them for participation in larger society—that is, to help them learn social skills necessary to secure reinforcement (Feldman & Wodarski, 1975; Sharry, 2008). For example, training in relaxation, systematic desensitization, assertiveness, and parenting skills can all occur in one-to-one contexts. From a social learning theory perspective, however, behavior is best learned in a group context, where greater generalization of the behavior to a broader variety of interactional contexts can occur. There are additional substantiated rationales for working with individuals in groups. Groups provide a context where new behaviors can be tested in a realistic atmosphere. Clients can receive immediate peer feedback regarding their problem-solving behaviors, and they are provided with role models to facilitate the acquisition of requisite social behavior.

These theoretical rationales indicate that treating clients in groups should facilitate the acquisition of socially relevant behaviors. However, criteria concerning who can benefit from group treatment need to be developed. Such knowledge will be forthcoming only when adequately designed research projects are executed in which clients are assigned randomly to individual and group treatment to control for confounding factors, such as type of behavior, age, gender, income level, and academic abilities.

In instances where an individual does not possess the necessary social behaviors to engage in a group, a one-to-one treatment relationship may be best. For example, many children with antisocial behaviors would be lost quickly in a group simply because they do not have the essential social behaviors for interaction. Likewise, with hyperactive children, it may be necessary to work on an individual basis until their behaviors are controlled enough to allow them to participate in a group context. As soon as they develop the necessary social skills, however, therapeutic changes are likely to be further facilitated if they can be placed in a group.

Generalization and Maintenance of Behavioral Change

Considerable study is needed to delineate those variables that facilitate the generalization and maintenance of behavior change. These may include substituting "naturally occurring" reinforcers, training relatives or other individuals in the client's environment, gradually removing or fading the contingencies, varying the conditions of training, using different schedules of reinforcement, and using delayed reinforcement and self-control procedures (Kazdin, 2000; Wodarski, 2009). Future sophisticated and effective social service delivery systems will employ such procedures.

Home visits, which were once the focus of practice, may also be employed in the future. Positive features of home visits include providing the opportunity to assess family interactions more adequately, increasing the probability of involving significant others in the treatment process, providing the opportunity to delineate attitudinal differences and their effect on therapy, increasing the worker's influence potential, and so on (Allen & Tracy, 2004; Beder, 1998).

Practice Recommendations

On the basis of the available data, the following generalizations may be made about treatment components:

1. Human services should be time limited.

2. Services should involve substantially structured roles for worker and client.

3. Techniques that have an accumulated base of research evidence should be utilized.

4. Appropriate intervention strategies (i.e., individual or group) should be used.

5. Behaviors acquired in clients as a result of therapy must be maintained once therapy concludes; therefore, appropriate maintenance procedures must be considered.

Macrolevel Interventions

If, following an assessment, a change agent decides that a client is exhibiting appropriate behaviors but that a treatment organization or institution is not providing adequate reinforcement for appropriate behaviors, or that it is punishing appropriate behavior, the change agent must then decide to engage in organizational or institutional change. This may mean working to change a social policy or alter an organization's culture and climate. The culture and climate of human services organizations have an impact on client outcomes (Hemmelgarn, Glisson, & James, 2006). Similarly, school climate has been shown to affect children's social, emotional, and cognitive development (Cohen & Geier, 2010).

In social work practice, the primary focus has been on changing the individual. Practitioners must restructure their thinking. "Inappropriate" behavior exhibited by a client must be examined according to who defined it as such and where requisite interventions should take place. Future research should provide various means of delineating how human behavior can be changed by interventions on different levels, thus providing the parameters for micro- and macrolevel interventions. The obvious question that will face social workers is how to coordinate these multilevel interventions (Goldfried & Davison, 1994).

Organizational Culture and Climate

Organizational culture and climate are defined in various ways in the literature and are sometimes used interchangeably. However, most of the literature points to climate as the psychological impact of the organizational environment on workers. The psychological climate is the individual's perception of the work environment, while organizational climate is the collective perception of the environment by all workers within the organization. Culture has more to do with behavioral expectations and norms within the organization. It encompasses the expectations for how workers perform their roles in the organization and the underlying values that drive those expectations (Glisson, Dukes, & Green, 2006).

Organizational culture and climate influence outcomes through their impact on clients, workers, and interventions (Franklin & Hopson, 2007). More positive cultures and climates are associated with less employee turnover, more positive attitudes toward their work, and higher-quality services (Glisson & James, 2002).

Research indicates that constructive organizational cultures, characterized by mutual support and respect, teamwork, and shared goals, support the use of new, innovative practices (Cooke & Szumal, 2000; Glisson, 2002; Hemmelgarn et al., 2006). A research-based intervention also is more likely to be implemented when practitioners and administrators view it as consistent with the organizational values and norms (Miller, 2001).

In addition to influencing readiness to implement new interventions, the organizational environment can directly influence client outcomes. In a study of organizational climate and interagency collaboration, Glisson and Hemmelgarn (1998) found that an organizational climate characterized by low conflict and cooperation predicted higher-quality services and improved psychosocial functioning among children served by such agencies.

Similarly, students from schools with open, collaborative cultures have better outcomes than those from schools with hierarchical cultures (Bowen, Rose, & Ware, 2006; Lee & Smith, 1993). Students also perform better in schools in which staff collaborate in decision making and share a common view of their mission (Harris & Hopkins, 2000; Hofman, Hofman, & Guldemong, 2001; Keys, Sharp, Greene, & Grayson, 2003).

Instruments have been developed to systematically assess social environmental characteristics of treatment contexts, particularly in mental hospitals. The instruments consist of scales designed to measure the dimensions of environmental contexts. One such scale is the Community-Oriented Program Environment Scale. This scale is designed to measure 10 dimensions of the treatment environment of psychiatric programs. These include staff and patient involvement, support, spontaneity, autonomy, practical orientation, personal problem orientation, anger and aggression, order and organization, program clarity, and staff control. The patients' and staff's perceptions of the extent of these dimensions in their program are measured. The scale has been found to be useful in the identification of factors that relate to favorable and unfavorable treatment outcomes, and to act as a feedback mechanism to facilitate social change and systems design (Bromet, Moos, & Bliss, 1976).

The Moos (1974) Standardized Ward Atmosphere Scale was developed and employed by Moos (1972) in his extensive examination of 15 Veterans Affairs hospitals. He and his colleagues attempted to discover the correlations between ward climate, as perceived by patients and staff, and treatment outcome, as defined by dropout rates, high turnover rates, and length-of-time-out-of-hospital rates. He found that certain items on the scale that were rated similarly by patients and staff correlated significantly with those particular outcomes:

1. Wards with high dropout rates were perceived as low in personal involvement and feelings of support on the part of either patients or staff and low in organization and clarity.

2. Wards with higher rapid-release rates were perceived as relatively well organized and clear, with moderately high staff control, but with little emphasis on open, spontaneous expression of feelings and little sense of support.

3. Wards most successful in helping patients remain out of the hospital were perceived as emphasizing patient autonomy and independence, being high in organization and clarity, and encouraging open expression of feelings, such as anger.

For assessing the learning environment in school settings, the School Success Profile–Learning Organization, developed by Gary Bowen (www.schoolsuccessprofile.org), provides a measure of learning organization characteristics. A learning organization is defined as a school that employs information from staff and key stakeholders to plan, implement, and evaluate practices that help students achieve desired outcomes. Actions and sentiments help define whether a school is a learning organization. Learning organizations are characterized by a team orientation, innovation, tolerance for error, and a results orientation. Sentiments characteristic of a learning organization include a sense of common purpose, respect, cohesion, trust, mutual support, and optimism (Bowen et al., 2006).

Practice Recommendations

Because the organizational culture and climate influence therapeutic outcomes, social workers will need skills in fostering a positive culture and climate. Some specific strategies include the following:

- Measure organizational characteristics, including climate and culture, and assess their impact on workers and clients.

- Facilitate collaboration and teamwork within agencies.

- Facilitate partnerships with other service providers in the community.

- Provide professional development on engaging families in organizations that serve children.

Overview

This chapter illustrates how research studies can be used to answer complex questions relevant to social work practice. These questions address client and worker characteristics that influence outcomes, as well as characteristics of the intervention and the organizational context in which the intervention is delivered. Including measures of these processes will be important for further developing our knowledge of effective social work practice.

Questions for Discussion

1. Discuss how you would make a decision about whether clients and clinicians should be matched by age, gender, race or ethnicity, or socioeconomic status.

2. Discuss how the use of research evidence relates to ethical social work practice.

3. You are working with a client whom you suspect would be more comfortable working with someone from his ethnic or cultural background. How would you proceed?

4. Describe some strategies you would use in the first session with a client to promote a strong therapeutic alliance.

5. How might a worker structure the physical space to be more conducive to forming a therapeutic alliance with clients?

References

Allen, S. F., & Tracy, E. M. (2004). Revitalizing the role of home visiting by school social workers. *Children and Schools, 26*(4), 197–208.

Attie, I., & Brooks-Gunn, J. (1987). Weight concerns as chronic stressors in women. In R. C. Barnett, L. Biener, & G. K. Baruch (Eds.), *Gender and stress* (pp. 218–254). New York: Free Press.

Beder, J. (1998). The home visit, revisited. *Families in Society, 79*(5), 514–522.

Blow, A. J., Timm, T. M., & Cox, R. (2008). The role of the therapist in therapeutic change: Does therapist gender matter? *Journal of Feminist Family Therapy, 20*(1), 66–86.

Bowen, G. L., Rose, R. A., & Ware, W. B. (2006). The reliability and validity of the School Success Profile Learning Organization Measure. *Evaluation and Program Planning, 29,* 97–104.

Bromet, E., Moos, R. H., & Bliss, F. (1976). The social climate of alcoholism treatment programs. *Archives of General Psychiatry, 33,* 910–916.

Centers for Disease Control and Prevention. (2009). *Suicide: Facts at a glance, summer 2009.* National Center for Injury Prevention and Control, CDC. Retrieved March 31, 2010, from http://www.cdc.gov/violenceprevention/pdf/Suicide-DataSheet-a.pdf

Cohen, J., & Geier, V. K. (2010). *School climate research summary, January 2010.* Retrieved from http://www.schoolclimate.org/climate/research.php

Colvin, J., Lee, M., Magnano, J., & Smith, V. (2008). The partners in prevention model: The evaluation and evolution of the task-centered case management model. *Research on Social Work Practice, 18*(6), 607–615.

Cooke, R. A., & Szumal, J. L. (2000). Using the Organizational Culture Inventory to understand the operating cultures of organizations. In N. M. Ashkanasy, C. P. M. Wilderom, & M. F. Peterson (Eds.), *Handbook of organizational culture and climate* (pp. 147–162). Thousand Oaks, CA: Sage.

Deaux, K. (1984). From individual differences to social categories: Analysis of a decade's research on gender. *American Psychologist, 39,* 105–116.

Feldman, R. A., & Wodarski, J. S. (1975). *Contemporary approaches to group treatment.* San Francisco: Jossey-Bass.

Field, C., & Caetano, R. (2010). The role of ethnic matching between patient and provider on the effectiveness of brief alcohol interventions with Hispanics. *Alcoholism: Clinical and Experimental Research, 34*(2), 262–271.

Fischer, J. (1978). *Effective casework practice.* New York: McGraw Hill.

Fisher, J. E., & O'Donohue, W. (Eds.). (2006). *Practitioners' guide to evidence-based psychotherapy.* New York: Kluwer Academic/Plenum.

Flicker, S. M., Waidron, H. B., Turner, C. W., Brody, J. L., & Hops, H. (2008). Ethnic matching and treatment outcome with Hispanic and Anglo substance-abusing adolescents in family therapy. *Journal of Family Psychology, 22*(3), 439–447.

Franklin, C., & Hopson, L. (2007). Facilitating the use of evidence-based practice in community organizations. *Journal of Social Work Education, 43*(3), 377–404.

Fraser, M. W., Kirby, L. D., & Smokowski, P. R. (2004). Risk and resilience in childhood. In M. W. Fraser (Ed.), *Risk and resilience in childhood: An ecological perspective* (pp. 13–66). Washington, DC: NASW Press.

Gellis, Z. D., McClive, K., & Brown, E. (2009). Treatments for depression in older persons with dementia. *Annals of Long Term Care, 17*(2), 29–36.

Giles, T. R., Prial, E. M., & Neims, D. M. (1993). Evaluating psychotherapies: A comparison of effectiveness; Special series: Evaluation in treatment methods in psychiatry. *International Journal of Mental Health, 22,* 43–65.

Glenn, M., & Kunnes, R. (1973). *Repression or revolution.* New York: Harper Colophon.

Glisson, C. (2002). The organizational context of children's mental health services. *Clinical Child and Family Psychology Review, 5*(4), 233–253.

Glisson, C., Dukes, D., & Green, P. (2006). The effects of the ARC organizational intervention on caseworker turnover, climate, and culture in children's service systems. *Child Abuse and Neglect, 30,* 855–880.

Glisson, C., & Hemmelgarn, A. (1998). The effects of organizational climate and interorganizational coordination on the quality and outcomes of children's service systems. *Child Abuse and Neglect, 22*(5), 401–421.

Glisson, C., & James, L. R. (2002). The cross-level effects of culture and climate in human service teams. *Journal of Organizational Behavior, 23*(6), 767–794.

Goldfried, M. R., & Davison, G. C. (1994). *Clinical behavior therapy.* New York: Wiley.

Halliday-Boykins, C. A., Schoenwald, S. K., & Letourneau, E. J. (2005). Caregiver–therapist ethnic similarity predicts youth outcomes from an empirically based treatment. *Journal of Consulting and Clinical Psychology, 73*(5), 808–818.

Hampton, B., Lambert, F. B., & Snell, W. R. (1986). Therapists' judgments of mentally healthy beliefs for women and men. *Journal of Rational-Emotive Therapy, 4,* 169–179.

Harris, A., & Hopkins, D. (2000). Introduction to special feature: Alternative perspectives on school improvement. *School Leadership and Management, 20*(1), 6–14.

Harrison, D. F., & Dziegielewski, S. F. (1992). Social work practice with the aged. In D. F. Harrison, J. S. Wodarski, & B. A. Thyer (Eds.), *Cultural diversity and social work practice* (pp. 181–213). Springfield, IL: Charles C Thomas.

Hemmelgarn, A. L., Glisson, C., & James, L. R. (2006). Organizational culture and climate: Implications for services and interventions research. *Clinical Psychology: Science and Practice, 13*(1), 73–89.

Henry, W. E., Sims, J. H., & Spray, S. L. (1971). *The fifth procession: Becoming a psychotherapist.* San Francisco: Jossey-Bass.

Henry, W. E., Sims, J. H., & Spray, S. L. (1973). *Public and private lives of psychotherapists.* San Francisco: Jossey-Bass.

Hofman, R. H., Hofman, W. H. A., & Guldemong, H. (2001). The effectiveness of cohesive schools. *International Journal of Leadership in Education, 4*(2), 115–135.

Horvath, A. O., & Bedi, R. P. (2002). The alliance. In J. C. Norcross (Ed.), *Psychotherapy relationships that work: Therapist contributions and responsiveness to patients* (pp. 37–69). New York: Oxford University Press.

Horvath, A. O., & Greenberg, L. S. (1989). Development and validation of the working alliance inventory. *Journal of Counseling Psychology, 36,* 223–233.

Jennings, L. R., & Davis, S. C. (1977). Attraction-enhancing client behaviors: A structures-learning approach for non-YAVIS. *Journal of Consulting and Clinical Psychology, 45,* 135–144.

Johnstone, B., Frank, R. G., Belar, C., Berk, S., Bieliauskas, L. A., Bigler, E. D., et al. (1995). Psychology in healthcare: Future directions. *Professional Psychology: Research and Practice, 26,* 341–365.

Kabacoff, R. I., Marwit, S. J., & Orlofsky, J. L. (1985). Correlates of sex-role stereotyping among mental health professionals. *Professional Psychology: Research and Practice, 16,* 98–105.

Kazdin, A. E. (2000). *Behavior modification in applied settings* (6th ed.). Belmont, CA: Wadsworth.

Keys, W., Sharp, C., Greene, K., & Grayson, H. (2003). *Successful leadership of schools in urban and challenging contexts: A review of the literature.* Nottingham: National College for School Leadership.

Kleinman, A., & Benson, P. (2006). Anthropology and the clinic: The problem of cultural competency and how to fix it. *PLoS Medicine, 3*(10), 1673–1676.

Kravetz, D., & Jones, L. E. (1981). Androgyny as a standard of mental health. *American Journal of Orthopsychiatry, 51,* 502–509.

Kropf, N. P., & Isaac, A. R. (1992). Cultural diversity and social work practice: An overview. In D. F. Harrison, J. S. Wodarski, & B. A. Thyer (Eds.), *Cultural diversity and social work practice* (pp. 3–12). Springfield: IL: Charles C Thomas.

Krug, E. G., Dahlberg, L. L., Mercy, J. A., Zwi, A., & Lozano, R. (2002). *World report on violence and health.* Geneva: World Health Organization.

Kumpfer, K. L., Alvarado, R., Smith, P., & Bellamy, N. (2002). Cultural sensitivity in universal family-based prevention interventions. *Prevention Science, 3*(3), 241–244.

Lee, V. E., & Smith, J. B. (1993). Effects of school restructuring on the achievement and engagement of middle-grade students. *Sociology of Education, 66,* 164–187.

Leland, J. (1982). Gender, drinking, and alcohol abuse. In I. Al-Issa (Ed.), *Gender and psychopathology* (pp. 201–236). New York: Academic.

Leventhal, A., & Martell, C. (2006). *The myth of depression as disease: Limitations and alternatives to drugs.* Westport, CT: Praeger.

Levine, M., & Perkins, D. V. (1987). *Principles of community psychology: Perspectives and applications.* New York: Oxford University Press.

Long, K., Homesley, L., & Wodarski, J. S. (2007). The role for social workers in the managed healthcare system: A model for empirically based psychosocial intervention. *Handbook of evidence-based social work practice in mental health* (2nd ed.). Hoboken, NJ: Wiley.

Manoleas, P. (1994). An outcome approach to assessing the cultural competence of MSW students. *Journal of Multicultural Social Work, 3*(1), 43–57.

Miller, R. L. (2001). Innovation in HIV prevention: Organizational and intervention characteristics affecting program adoption. *American Journal of Community Psychology, 29,* 621–647.

Moos, R. H. (1972). Size, staffing, and psychiatric ward treatment environment. *Archives of General Psychiatry, 26,* 414–418.

Moos, R. H. (1974). *Ward Atmosphere Scale manual.* Palo Alto, CA: Consulting Psychologist Press.

Myers, J. K., Weissman, M. M, Tischler, G. L., Holzer, C. E., Leaf, P. J., Orvaschel, H., et al. (1984). Six-month prevalence of psychiatric disorders in three communities. *Archives of General Psychiatry, 41,* 959–967.

Nam, S. K., Chu, H. J., Lee, M. K., Lee, J. H., Kim, N., & Lee, S. M. (2010). A meta-analysis of gender differences in attitudes toward seeking professional psychological help. *Journal of American College Health, 59*(2), 110–116.

Nicholson, J., Dine-Young, S., Simon, L., Fisher, W. H., & Bateman, A. (1996). Impact of Medicaid managed care on child and adolescent emergency mental health screening in Massachusetts. *Psychiatric Services, 47,* 1344–1350.

Norcross, J. C. (Ed.). (2002). *Psychotherapy relationships that work: Therapist contributions and responsiveness to patient needs.* New York: Oxford University Press.

Norcross, J. C., & Hill, C. E. (2004). Empirically supported therapy relationships. *Clinical Psychologist, 57*(3), 19–24.

Nugent, W. R., & Halvorson, H. (1995). Testing the effects of active listening. *Research on Social Work Practice, 5*(2), 152–175.

Padilla, A. M., & Perez, W. (2003). Acculturation, social identity, and social cognition: A new perspective. *Hispanic Journal of Behavioral Sciences, 25*(1), 35–55.

Paris, M., Bedregal, L., Añez, L., Shahar, G., & Davidson, L. (2004). Psychometric properties of the Spanish version of the therapeutic collaboration scale (TCS). *Hispanic Journal of Behavioral Sciences, 26*(3), 390–402.

Perry, R., & Limb, G. E. (2004). Ethnic/racial matching of clients and social workers in public child welfare. *Children and Youth Services Review, 26*(10), 965–979.

Prochaska, J. O. (1996). A stage paradigm for integrating clinical and public health approaches to smoking cessation. *Addictive Behaviors, 21,* 721–732.

Prochaska, J. O., & DiClemente, C. C. (1982). Transtheoretical therapy: Towards a more integrative model of change. *Psychotherapy Theory Research and Practice, 19,* 276–288.

Ramnerö, J., & Öst, L. G. (2007). Panic and avoidance in panic disorder with agoraphobia: Clinical relevance of change in different aspects of the disorder. *Journal of Behavior Therapy and Experimental Psychiatry, 38*(1), 29–39.

Reid, W. J. (1978). *The task-centered system.* New York: Columbia University Press.

Reid, W. J. (1997). Research on task-centered practice. *Social Work Research, 21*(3), 132–137.

Reid, W. J., & Epstein, L. (1972). *Task-centered casework.* New York: Columbia University Press.

Reid, W. J., & Epstein, L. (1977). *Task-centered practice.* New York: Columbia University Press.

Ricker, M., Nystul, M., & Waldo, M. (1999). Counselors' and clients' ethnic similarity and therapeutic alliance in time-limited outcomes of counseling. *Psychological Reports, 84,* 674–676.

Robins, L. N., Helzer, J. F., Weissman, M. M., Orvaschel, H., Gruenberg, E., Burke, J. D., et al. (1984). Lifetime prevalence of specific psychiatric disorders in three sites. *Archives of General Psychiatry, 41,* 949–958.

Rosenthal, R. (1976). *Experimenter effects in behavioral research.* New York: Irvington.

Ryan, W. (1971). *Blaming the victim.* New York: Vintage.

Scaturo, D. J. (2010). A tripartite learning conceptualization of psychotherapy: The therapeutic alliance, technical interventions, and relearning. *American Journal of Psychotherapy, 64*(1), 1–27.

Schaffer, K. F. (1981). *Sex roles and human behavior.* Cambridge, MA: Winthrop.

Schinke, S., Brounstein, P., & Gardner, S. (2002). *Science-based prevention programs and principles, 2002.* Rockville, MD: Center for Substance Abuse Prevention, Substance Abuse and Mental Health Services Administration.

Schofield, W. (1964). *Psychotherapy: The purchase of friendships.* Englewood Cliffs, NJ: Prentice Hall.

Seabury, B. A. (1980). Communication problems in social work practice. *Social Work, 25,* 40–43.

Sharry, J. (2008). *Solution-focused groupwork.* Thousand Oaks, CA: Sage.

Shealy, C. G. (1995). From *Boys Town* to *Oliver Twist:* Separating fact from fiction in welfare reform and out-of-home placement of children and youth. *American Psychologist, 50,* 565–580.

Specht, H., & Courtney, M. (1993). *Fallen angels.* New York: Free Press.

Thyer, B. A., & Wodarski, J. S. (2007). *Handbook of evidence-based social work practice in mental health.* Hoboken, NJ: Wiley.

Thyer, B. A., Wodarski, J. S., Myers, L. L., & Harrison, D. F. (2010). *Cultural diversity and social work practice.* Springfield, IL: Charles C Thomas.

Tinsley, H. E., & Harris, D. J. (1976). Client expectations for counseling. *Journal of Counseling Psychology, 23,* 173–177.

Travis, C. B. (1988). *Women and health psychology: Mental health issues.* Hillsdale, NJ: Erlbaum.

Van Wormer, K. (2007). Principles of motivational interviewing geared to stages of change: A pedagogical challenge. *Journal of Teaching in Social Work, 27*(1/2), 21–35.

Weger, H., Castle, G. R., & Emmett, M. C. (2010). Active listening in peer interviews: The influence of message paraphrasing on perceptions of listening skills. *International Journal of Listening, 24*(1), 34–49.

Werner-Wilson, R. J., Michaels, M. L., Thomas, S. G., & Thiesen, A. M. (2003). Influence of therapist behaviors on therapeutic alliance. *Contemporary Family Therapy, 25*(4), 381–390.

Whitley, R. (2009). The implications of race and ethnicity for shared decision making. *Psychiatric Rehabilitation Journal, 32,* 227–230.

Widom, C. S. (Ed.). (1984). *Sex roles and psychopathology.* New York: Plenum.

Wintersteen, M. B., Mensinger, J. L., & Diamond, G. S. (2005). Do gender and racial differences affect early therapeutic alliance and treatment retention in adolescents? *Professional Psychology: Research and Practice, 36,* 400–408.

Wodarski, J. S. (1994). Cognitive and behavioral treatment: Uses, issues, and future directions. In D. K. Granvold (Ed.), *Cognitive and behavioral treatment: Methods and applications.* Belmont, CA: Wadsworth.

Wodarski, J. S. (2009). *Behavioral medicine: A social worker's guide.* New York: Routledge.

Wodarski, J. S., & Hilarski, C. (2006). Comprehensive mental health practice with sex offenders and their families. London: Routledge.

Planning for Conducting Research in Community Agencies

The previous chapters have provided a discussion of evidence-based practice and the use of research to inform practice. This chapter addresses practical aspects of planning and implementing research in social service agencies. Whether you are a practitioner in an agency who needs to evaluate the effectiveness of interventions or a researcher who is evaluating an agency's services, understanding the dynamics within the agency that affect your research is a critical first step. In this chapter, a practitioner who is working to evaluate his or her own practices or interventions delivered within an agency is called an evidence-based practitioner. An evaluator is someone who contracts with the agency to evaluate its services but is not employed by the agency.

SECURING PRACTITIONER AGREEMENT FOR EVALUATION OF PRACTICE

Many practitioners have concerns about being evaluated. These concerns can be alleviated by providing rationales for the evaluation, having both workers and supervisors participate in the process and choose items for evaluation, indicating the types of procedures to be evaluated, and deciding mechanisms for the evaluation.

Professionals who must evaluate should be prepared to provide rationale as to its benefits and to answer such questions as, Could evaluation be detrimental to the formation of the relationship between client and social worker? Will as much improvement take place in the client as would occur if evaluation were omitted? Can the data be used to discredit my practice? Staff members must be assured that the evaluation will not be used to criticize any worker or portray anyone in a negative light but that it will be implemented to provide the worker necessary feedback on practice behavior, with the ultimate goal of improving services provided to clients.

One technique for reducing the amount of anxiety over being evaluated is to have all workers, including supervisors, participate in the evaluation. Additionally, workers should participate in the choice of criteria used in the evaluation of performances (e.g., the amount of client improvement or change on agreed outcome measures) and the means of evaluation (e.g., video and/or audio recording, behavioral observation, interview schedules, or self-inventories). What will be evaluated and how it will be evaluated must be clearly outlined prior to the initiation of evaluation. Keep in mind, too, that evaluation procedures are most readily executed when they are unobtrusive and guarantee anonymity and confidentiality.

Specific factors that may lead to the ready acceptance of evaluation in an agency include the agency's executive support of evaluation to improve practice, the encouragement offered by individuals implementing the evaluation, the professional manner employed by those executing the process, and inclusion of the executive's requisite job performance in the evaluation. The review of worker competency must be handled in the highest possible professional manner. Positive criticism offered professionally can lead to improved practice; criticism offered degradingly will not. How the evaluation process is executed and how various professionals treat the information for improving practice skills is dependent on developing mutual relationships among the individuals using the data. These collegial relationships should be characterized by mutual trust, sharing, respect, encouragement, and acceptance, with the goal of improving services provided to clients.

INSTITUTIONAL REVIEW BOARDS

Conducting research typically requires approval from an institutional review board (IRB), a group of independent professionals whose purpose is to ensure that the research procedures are ethical and research participants are protected from harm. Universities and agencies receiving federal funding require that researchers submit project summaries to an IRB before commencing research procedures. School boards and community agencies often have their own IRBs. A collaborative project in which a university researcher administers a questionnaire to high school students is likely to require approval from both the university and school board IRBs. This process may take several months because each IRB may request modifications before approving the research.

The IRB may request that modifications to a project be made in order to meet its ethical standards. Such modifications may include

- providing a more detailed description of research procedures, including possible benefits and risks to participants, in the consent form;

- clearly stating the procedures for approaching potential participants, explaining the purpose of the study, and requesting their participation;

- adding a provision for referring participants to appropriate services when needs are identified during the course of the study; and

- justifying the study's sample size.

Some studies may qualify for an expedited review, in which the project can be approved without the review of the full board. Studies that may be exempt from needing full board approval include those in which procedures are part of normal educational practices, those that rely on existing data, and observations of public behavior in which the participants' confidentiality is protected, among others. Each IRB may have slightly different standards regarding exemptions, so it is important to consult the IRB(s) that will be reviewing your study for specific exemption criteria.

THE ASSESSMENT OF AGENCY CHARACTERISTICS

Before undertaking research in a community-based agency, it is necessary to spend sufficient time within the agency to learn what research questions can be addressed within that context and to build trust with key agency personnel so they are comfortable with evaluation procedures (Cunningham & Duffee, 2009). During this period, the evidence-based practitioner or evaluator should determine the research interests of administrators and other practitioners in the agency so he or she can incorporate into the evaluation research questions that are valued by many key stakeholders. It is also helpful to align the research questions with the priorities of any funders of program services. A study formulated this way is likely to earn essential support from the administration and line staff, as well as remaining consonant with the interests of any involved funding agencies and the social worker's own empirical concerns. Most successful studies meet the agency's goals, the funding agency's objectives, and the practitioner's own interests. In effect, then, if other individuals are to be involved in the research, the initial stages of the research must be devoted to mutually validated research objectives.

In the initial appraisal, it is essential that the evidence-based practitioner or evaluator weigh the benefits of a methodologically strong research design with the resources required to implement different designs. In considering the design, assessing whether sufficient control can be exercised over variables that might confound the study is important. Another important consideration is whether the agency has sufficient resources to meet the demands of a research design. For example, randomly assigning participants to either an intervention or control group controls for extraneous variables, or any factor other than the intervention that may explain participant outcomes. However, for a number of reasons, random assignment is not always feasible in community agencies. It may not be possible to randomly assign clients to groups within an agency. For example, youths in residential treatment typically belong to a house in which they work with a range of personnel on developing social and problem-solving skills. The agency is unlikely to randomly assign these youths to houses for the purpose of evaluating the practices in a particular house. Many clinicians and administrators have ethical concerns about random assignment because of the potential for subjecting some clients to an ineffective intervention or withholding an intervention so clients can be part of a control group. If random assignment is not feasible or appropriate in an agency, the evidence-based practitioner should determine whether a different research design can provide valid and trustworthy answers to the research questions.

Similarly, agency personnel may have concerns about baseline periods used to measure a presenting problem before an intervention is provided. Establishing a baseline can be important in evaluating the effects of an intervention, though it entails withholding a particular mode of treatment for a limited period of time. The application of baseline periods has proven to be particularly valuable in assessing the differential effects of one or more treatments immediately pursuant to the baseline.

Practitioners need support during the period of a study when no treatment interventions are employed. They may worry about the ethical implications of delaying the intervention in order to obtain baseline data. Clinicians may worry that the clients' needs are being neglected during the baseline phase. However, in many cases, the use of a baseline can be justified because it allows clinicians to compare clients' functioning during the intervention with their functioning without the intervention. They are, thus, enabling the practitioners to better assess whether the intervention is helpful for the clients.

Evidence-based practitioners and external evaluators must evaluate the extent to which agency personnel will be involved in the study and must secure the agency personnel's commitment before the study's inception. This procedure is essential in any research project but is particularly necessary if the study is to place significant demands on staff time. In the planning stages, it is often difficult to estimate the amount of time that will be required of agency practitioners and other staff. In order to secure their informed and sincere commitment, the time commitments are outlined ahead of time so agency personnel can make an informed decision about participating in a study. The evidence-based practitioner or evaluator also should indicate that additional time may be required as the study evolves but that, preferably, such decisions will be made in conjunction with the pertinent staff. Although most of the activities mentioned above are essential for the successful execution of an empirical research study, these particular activities are especially crucial because they occur early in the research process and, as a result, serve to define the various opportunities and constraints that will determine the project's long-term success. The amount of time spent dealing with these issues depends on the complexity of the research study. For example, a single-case study design is easier to implement than a classical experimental procedure in staff time, administrative coordination, and financial resources.

COORDINATION OF THE RESEARCH

If the agency staff and evidence-based practitioner or evaluator meet early enough to define their various goals and responsibilities, coordination of the research should be relatively uncomplicated. The various responsibilities of those who will be involved with the evaluation should be defined clearly and promptly. In the case of an external evaluation, explicit statements should be made regarding to whom the evaluator is accountable. Confusion and ambiguity regarding accountability can produce ill feelings that may deter the research. The process of defining accountability and responsibility must be handled delicately because, in some instances, agency executives may wish the employed researchers to integrate with the agency to such an extent that they lose their autonomy.

READINESS FOR CHANGE

The previous chapter discussed organizational culture and climate and their effect on client outcomes. Organizational culture and climate also have been found to have important implications for the success of implementing and evaluating an intervention (Cooke & Szumal, 2000; Glisson, 2002; Jaskyte & Dressler, 2005; Shortell, Bennett, & Byck, 1998). Practitioners and administrators are more likely to adopt new practices and procedures when they are consistent with organizational values and cultural norms (Miller, 2001). Conducting some type of organizational assessment before implementing a new intervention is important in order to avoid expending valuable time and resources effecting new practices the organization is unlikely to sustain (Franklin & Hopson, 2007). Standardized measures of organizational culture that may be helpful in this process include the Organizational Culture Survey (Glisson & James, 2002), the Organizational Culture Inventory (Cooke & Szumal, 2000), and, for school settings, the School Success Profile–Learning Organization (Bowen, Rose, & Ware, 2006).

Standardized measures are available to assess organizational characteristics that can help identify whether the administration and practitioners are ready to take on a new intervention and research procedures for the evaluation process. *Readiness for change* is a term used to describe the extent to which an organization has the capacity and motivation to incorporate new practices and procedures. If evaluators measure readiness for change prior to beginning study procedures, they will have a better understanding of potential barriers to effective implementation and evaluation. In response to this need, researchers have developed reliable and valid measures of readiness for change (Cunningham et al., 2002; Lehman, Greener, & Simpson, 2002). The Organizational Readiness for Change Scale (Lehman et al., 2002) and the Evidence-Based Practice Attitudes Scale (Aarons, 2004) are two instruments that are useful for assessing readiness for change and attitudes toward adopting new practices.

INTERPRETATION OF THE RESEARCH TO THE AGENCY STAFF

Most research investigations involve a substantial proportion of agency personnel, whose commitment to the research is essential for its completion. To secure the necessary commitment, research practitioners should be able to discuss major aspects of the research, emphasizing the importance of staff cooperation for the execution and completion of the project. In social work agencies, naturally, an emphasis on service aspects of the study may be more appealing to staff than emphasis on its research attributes. Preferably, however, professional staff should realize that the two activities need not be mutually exclusive and, indeed, usually should proceed in conjunction with each other. For example, a school social worker may want to conduct an assessment of student perceptions of school climate and whether these perceptions are associated with academic performance. In selling this idea to administrators and teachers, the social worker will need to explain why the findings of this study are relevant to their work and how they will help them achieve their goals for teaching and learning. The social worker may need to cite research that connects school climate with academic outcomes. Also helpful is communicating feasible strategies for improving school climate should the assessment reveal a need for intervention.

It is often necessary to defend or explain questions regarding the research. In these instances, the evidence-based practitioner also serves as an educator. The question "What can be gained from the study?" can best be handled by indicating that the practitioner's and researchers' ultimate goals are actually quite similar: to help clients function adequately. In describing procedures such as random assignment, for example, explaining the rationale underlying randomization in terms that relate to improving services to clients will be important. Since random assignment may allow for a more trustworthy answer to questions about the effectiveness of services, this information will be more useful in informing service delivery than in other designs.

CHOICE OF TERMS

Because some words have different connotations to practitioners and researchers, successful execution of the research study sometimes depends on the choice of terms used to communicate various features of the study. These can include semantic labels, such as "control group," "randomness," "antisocial child," or "behavior modification." When introducing such labels, evidence-based practitioners should be certain that there is a clear understanding of the terms so workers do not assign incorrect or unintended meanings to them. The same procedures should be used in the interpretation of a research project to lay boards and citizens of the general community. A misinterpretation once occurred, for example, when a treatment method labeled "behavior modification" was presented to the staff of a community center. Workers immediately responded with certain perceptions that indicated they viewed such treatment to include the "shocking" of children and similar punitive measures. Clear explication of the method used was necessary for the workers to understand its goals and implementation. For instance, it was explained that group leaders using behavior modification were taught primarily to avoid punitive measures and, instead, to set rewards for certain behaviors or decrease others by not attending to them.

PROCEDURES THAT ENHANCE INTERVENTION FIDELITY

Much of the literature focuses on the importance of fidelity in implementing research-based interventions. *Fidelity* refers to implementation of an intervention as originally intended. Research supports the idea that interventions implemented with fidelity have better outcomes than those in which implementers diverge from protocols (Blakely et al., 1987; Botvin, 2004; Elliott & Mihalic, 2004). In most cases, interventions implemented in community settings are not implemented with fidelity (Castro, Barrera, & Martinez, 2004; Rohrbach, Grana, Sussman, & Valente, 2006). Reasons for poor fidelity include lack of training and support, inadequate resources, low morale and burnout among personnel, and insufficient time (Botvin, 2004). Some strategies for promoting fidelity include training, supervision, and ongoing technical assistance in implementing the intervention (Franklin & Hopson, 2007).

Consistent supervision is important for promoting intervention fidelity. The effectiveness of an intervention is influenced by whether supervisors are consistent in their supervision of the workers involved in its implementation. Consistency of supervision can be achieved by conducting intensive training sessions for each method and through frequent and uniform monitoring of supervisory activity. Forms can be developed to serve as uniform guides and records for supervisory sessions. Videos and observations of intervention sessions can also be used during supervision meetings to assess for the quality of implementation.

Any study also must have safeguards against artifacts to which the results can be falsely attributed. In one example in which an evaluation depended on bringing 150 children into the agency, it was necessary to obtain data on absences to assess for clients' attendance to group sessions. Likewise, it was deemed essential to engage in first-hand observations of the behavior of both workers and clients within the groups. Periodic checks on supervisors' sessions and workers' meetings with their groups were needed. Monitoring procedures are most readily executed when they are unobtrusive, guarantee anonymity and confidentiality, and are based on the informed consent of participants. To our pleasant surprise, monitoring procedures were readily accepted by all participants in the research, including the children, once the above considerations were addressed. Observers were trained to remain relatively inconspicuous; safeguards were devised to ensure the confidentiality of data; and, most important, the approval of participants was solicited and granted before beginning the monitoring procedures.

Few agencies have considered the key organizational requirements for the evaluation of social work services. Most agencies are poorly structured for the delivery or evaluation of practice. This problem limits the information on how services are being implemented, which prohibits the evaluation and feedback workers need to become competent and provide effective service. For example, few agencies provide observation areas with one-way mirrors where workers can observe one another and isolate effective techniques for working with a child or his or her family unit. Viewing areas enable the unobtrusive gathering of samples of a child's behavior and make easy the recording of interactions between parents and child. Observation areas can facilitate training programs where parents learn to change interactional patterns with their child and can provide means by which parents can view and model therapist behaviors exhibited during work with the child. These features also may enable workers to secure necessary data for the systematic evaluation of therapeutic services. This feedback enables workers to sharpen their practice skills.

Video recordings can provide an effective and reliable medium to evaluate therapeutic services. Many benefits are accrued by using video recordings to evaluate social work practice. Video recording provides a medium through which client–worker interactions can be accurately recorded by capturing more verbal details, such as association and clustering of words; duration of utterances; number of interruptions; questions; summary and interpretative statements; length of silent periods; and such nonverbal details as posture, gestures, eye contact, and touching. Likewise, with proper analysis, the video recordings can sharpen practice skills and lead to an understanding of how behaviors exhibited by clients and workers influence their mutual interaction. Also, video recordings may be used as training vehicles for new and established workers, as educational devices for the community at large and for other agencies in staff screening procedures, as documentation of important decisions made by executives, as a permanent record for current and future research activities, and in many other valuable capacities.

An agency should determine whether video recording sessions improves service to clients. In assessing the quality of client–worker interactions, the criteria can be stated in the following questions: Are worker practice behaviors changing in aspects of relationship formation and employment of change techniques? Are client behaviors changing more readily in desired directions by employing video recordings? Is the agency saving the worker's time through decreasing the amount of time spent on traditional audio recording, thus providing more time for the worker to interact with the client?

Preferably, the agency should set up organizational procedures for recording and viewing of various social work practices. If there is no specified place for viewing the tapes, it may decrease the chances that viewings of the video recordings will be used to evaluate the quality of implementation. Therefore, it is suggested that an agency provide a specific area where the tapes can be easily viewed; such an area might be designated the "practice skills center."

The optimal length of recordings for review is approximately 20 minutes. Periods longer than that may overwhelm practitioners because of the large amount of information. In the initial stages of viewing, practitioners must discuss the criteria on which the tapes will be reviewed. After viewing a few, they can decide to record entire meetings or certain portions. Likewise, other aspects of taping—such as whether the camera should focus only on the worker or the client, or on both, or what portion of the body should be taped—can be reviewed.

Staff Concerns Regarding Observation

Staff will have concerns about the use of video recordings in evaluating their practice. Most of these concerns can be handled by indicating the types of procedures that will be evaluated and assuring them that the video recordings will not be used to criticize any one worker or portray a worker in a negative light but will be implemented only to improve services provided to clients. One technique for reducing anxiety about being recorded is to have all workers and supervisors participate. However, how the person produces the tape and how the various supervisors utilize it for improving practice skills will be dependent on developing mutual relationships among persons using the tapes. These collegial relationships should be characterized by mutual trust, sharing, respect, encouragement, and acceptance, with the goal of improving services provided to clients. Criticism offered professionally can lead to improved practice; degrading criticism will not enable one to tap the potential of taping to improve practice. Finally, procedures are best executed when they are unobtrusive and guarantee confidentiality.

Factors that may lead to the acceptance of video recordings to improve practice include the encouragement offered by the individuals making the recordings and the professional manner of those executing the process. Professionals who want to use video recordings may need to offer rationales as to its benefits and answer questions such as, Could the video recordings be detrimental to the formation of the relationship between client and worker? Will client improvement be affected? Can the recordings be used to discredit my practice?

Potential Benefits of Video Recording to Agencies

1. Improvement of social work practice may be accomplished through video recording. Recent research indicates that after viewing video recordings, therapists are more willing to accept their deficiencies and concentrate on improving them, are more receptive to new techniques, and are more aware of their verbal and nonverbal presence.

2. Video recordings provide a medium through which the quality of the social services being offered to clients can be monitored.

3. Video recordings provide a permanent record for research that can be used by the agency to improve practice and contribute to the knowledge of social work practice.

4. Records of important decisions made by the agency administration are readily available. If controversy develops regarding the decisions, a permanent record is available to provide the rationale for the decision and clarify discrepancies.

5. Various recordings can be made to efficiently demonstrate regular practice skills necessary for training social workers. This saves time for the practitioner who normally must explain these regular skills to each new worker.

USE OF EVALUATION DATA TO IMPROVE PRACTICE

Evaluation data can be used to improve practice competencies through (a) pinpointing the worker's behaviors that need to be altered, (b) measuring the frequency of such behaviors, (c) developing a program to alter the worker's behavior, and (d) providing the worker with feedback on targeted behaviors. Video recording client and worker interactions should facilitate isolation of those behaviors that need to be altered and likewise provide the opportunity for supervisors to reinforce the worker's favorable practice behavior.

Table 4.1 illustrates 14 micro- and macrolevel competencies, along with the criteria for evaluation and pertinent data that might be used in the assessment of a residential treatment program for children. For example, a macrolevel competency would be the agency's implementation of a training program for new staff to introduce the theoretical practice model being employed. Criteria to evaluate this competency would be number of staff-development activities, money allocated to such activities, and initial orientation procedures. Data would include the assessment of the competency budget, training manuals, the number of training sessions, and record of staff participation in such activities.

TABLE 4.1 Competencies, Criteria, and Data for Assessing Worker Behavior in a Residential Treatment Center for Children

Competency	Criteria	Data
A clearly defined targeted population	Specify client population in terms of number of children accommodated, age, gender, behavior problems	Policy statement, descriptive survey
A clearly defined theoretical model validated through research—that is, behavioral group work and token economy	A policy statement reflecting the competency, staff development programs geared toward theory, testing the staff's knowledge of theory and practice techniques, behavioral observations of practice	Inspection of treatment plans (case records to see if the plan follows from theory), observation of staff behavior
Training program to orient staff toward practice model and philosophy used in the agency	Number and types of staff development activities within the agency, money allocated in the budget for staff development, initial orientation to agency in terms of the model of practice	Budget, training manual, the number of training sessions held, a record of participation in staff development programs
Clearly defined job description—that is, tasks to be performed by different levels of workers	Specify level of training for each task, type and years of experience, skills needed for job	Job requirements, how often they are updated
An individualized treatment plan with criteria for measuring change for each child	Are there individualized treatment goals and a specified treatment program for meeting these goals? They should include a time frame, behavioral objectives, and specified activity, or all those involved in treatment and outcome specifications.	Case records, behavioral observations
Direct family involvement with child in treatment	A specified number of family sessions, a family assessment, a family treatment program	Treatment plan, case records of staff time in terms of who they see and what they do
A contingent environment individualized for each child	Is staff behavior in accordance with theoretical model? For example, are reinforcers given for desired behavior?	Treatment plan, behavioral observations, videotaping of therapeutic environment

Encouragement of community contact and public education	Number and types of community activities in which residents participate, number and types of residential treatment center activities in which community members participate, number and types of activities geared toward public education brochures, speakers for community groups, etc.	A list of the activities in which residents and community members participated, compared with an ideal standard of participation for such activities
Provision of adequate schooling	Are all children attending an accredited school or one with accreditation pending?	Case records
Assessment of overall treatment success	There is a prespecified proportion of children who meet the outcome criteria in order for the program to be considered successful	Policy statement containing this proportion, case records of the proportion of clients with successful outcomes against those not successful
Valid discharge criteria	Individualized reasons for discharging the child to the previous home, a new home—that is, a foster home, a different community agency, etc. This should be based on the child's and the family's progress.	Case records
Post-discharge follow-up	Has the achieved outcome been maintained for a specified interval (i.e., monthly, for 6 months, at 1 year, and at 2 years)?	Follow-up studies to see if behavior is maintained
The coordination of services among agencies involved with the child and the family	A centralized program for all children's services. In lieu of this, residential treatment centers can have a staff liaison to establish and facilitate communication among agencies. This person should act as a resource person for therapists who could then continue treatment with the family.	Job descriptions
Returning the child to the community as quickly as possible	As behavior moves toward the desired goals, the child's environment should be expanded to include increasingly longer home visits, progressing from partial residency to full residency. Therapist, family, and child should be involved in this planning.	Case records, record of movement toward community placement—that is, number and length of home visits

Questions for Discussion

1. What are some agency characteristics that are important to examine as part of an evaluation? Why are they important to include in the evaluation?

2. How would you collect follow-up data to examine long-term outcomes for adults who received substance abuse treatment services? What purpose would the follow-up data serve?

References

Aarons, G. A. (2004). Mental health provider attitudes toward adoption of evidence-based practice: The Evidence-Based Practice Attitude Scale (EBPAS). *Mental Health Services Research, 6*(2), 61–74.

Botvin, G. J. (2004). Advancing prevention science and practice: Challenges, critical issues, and future directions. *Prevention Science, 5*(1), 69–72.

Blakely, C. H., Mayer, J. P., Gottschalk, R. G., Schmitt, N., Davidson, W. S., Roitman, D. B., et al. (1987). The fidelity-adaptation debate: Implications for the implementation of public sector social programs. *American Journal of Community Psychology, 15*(3), 253–268.

Bowen, G. L., Rose, R. A., & Ware, W. B. (2006). The reliability and validity of the School Success Profile–Learning Organization Measure. *Evaluation and Program Planning, 29,* 97–104.

Castro, F. G., Barrera, M., & Martinez, C. R. (2004). The cultural adaptation of prevention interventions: Resolving tensions between fidelity and fit. *Prevention Science, 5*(1), 41–45.

Cooke, R. A., & Szumal, J. L. (2000). Using the Organizational Culture Inventory to understand the operating cultures of organizations. In N. M. Ashkanasy, C. P. M. Wilderom, & M. F. Peterson (Eds.), *Handbook of organizational culture and climate* (pp. 147–162). Thousand Oaks, CA: Sage.

Cunningham, C. E., Woodward, C. A., Shannon, H. S., MacIntosh, J., Lendrum, B., Rosenbloom, D., et al. (2002). Readiness for organizational change: A longitudinal study of workplace, psychological, and behavioural correlates. *Journal of Occupational and Organizational Psychology, 75*(4), 377–392.

Cunningham, S., & Duffee, D. E. (2009). Styles of evidence-based practice in the child welfare system. *Evidence-based social work, 6*(2), 176–197.

Elliott, D., & Mihalic, S. (2004). Issues in disseminating and replicating effective prevention programs. *Prevention Science, 5,* 47–53.

Franklin, C., & Hopson, L. (2007). New challenges in research: Translating community-based practices into evidence-based practices. *Journal of Social Work Education, 43*(3), 377–404.

Glisson, C. (2002). The organizational context of children's mental health services. *Clinical Child and Family Psychology Review, 5*(4), 233–252.

Glisson, C., & James, L. R. (2002). The cross-level effects of culture and climate in human services teams. *Journal of Organizational Behavior, 23,* 767–794.

Jaskyte, K., & Dressler, W. (2005). Organizational culture and innovation in nonprofit human service organizations. *Administration in Social Work, 29*(2), 23–41.

Lehman, W. E. K., Greener, J. M., & Simpson, D. D. (2002). Assessing organizational readiness for change. *Journal of Substance Abuse Treatment, 22*(4), 197–209.

Miller, R. L. (2001). Innovation in HIV prevention: Organizational and intervention characteristics affecting program adoption. *American Journal of Community Psychology, 29,* 621–647.

Rohrbach, L. A., Grana, R., Sussman, S., & Valente, T. W. (2006). Type II translation: Transporting prevention interventions from research to real-world settings. *Evaluation in the Health Professions, 29*(3), 302–333.

Shortell, S. M., Bennett, C. L., & Byck, G. R. (1998). Assessing the impact of continuous quality improvement on clinical practice: What it will take to accelerate progress. *Milbank Quarterly, 76,* 593–624.

CHAPTER 5

Choice of Outcome Measures and Means for Assessment

Previous chapters have addressed how research can be used to help the practitioner provide better services to clients. The chapters to follow cover basic research methodology, designs, and statistics needed for practitioners to begin using research in their empirical practice.

CLIENT OUTCOMES

The first requisite for the use of research in practice is the delineation of the possible outcomes for the client with whom the clinician is working. The specification of outcomes is critical because they determine what data will be measured and what criteria will be needed to evaluate an empirical intervention (Wodarski & Feit, 2009). Discussions with other professionals about the appropriateness of various outcomes and an adequate review of the available literature help make possible the elucidation of outcomes. From the discussion in Chapter 1, it is evident that professional and client values, theoretical orientation, agency goals, social-political factors, societal factors, available resources, and practice context affect the chosen outcomes.

Once outcomes are decided, the basic question is how to measure them. Basically, there are four means of collecting the necessary data: behavioral observations, standardized scales, self-inventories, and interviews. Four critical questions must be asked of the methodology chosen: (1) Can the necessary data be secured reliably? (2) How costly, in terms of time, money, energy, and administration, is it to secure the data needed? (3) How comfortable is the client with the chosen method of data collection? (4) How relevant is the chosen method for providing answers to the main question(s) guiding practice decisions, as discussed in Chapter 1?

MEASURES OF WORKER AND CLIENT BEHAVIOR

Various measures such as interview schedules, checklists filled out by clients and significant others (e.g., group leaders, parents, referral agencies, grandparents), and behavioral observations (e.g., time-sampling schedules) can be used to assess change in clients. Likewise, behavioral rating scales can be used to assess the behaviors exhibited by the worker. Excellent publications are available that describe the various measures that can be used (e.g., Bloom, Fischer, & Orme, 2009; Fischer & Corcoran, 2007). They specify particular items included in each measure, appropriate clientele, types of data provided, reliability, and procedures involved in administration. The type of measurement process selected depends on the behaviors chosen for modification; availability of technical equipment; cost of securing various types of data; context of measurement; and frequency, duration, and intensity of the target behavior. The focus in this chapter is on the general features that should be considered essential to any measure chosen for practice evaluation. Fischer and Corcoran (2007) provide a series of rapid-assessment measures relevant for a wide range of populations and presenting problems in the public domain.

CRITERIA FOR EVALUATION MEASURES

Reliability

When choosing a particular measure, the practitioner should ask two questions: Is the measure reliable, and is it valid? *Reliability* refers to the consistency of the measure. If used repeatedly under the same conditions, a reliable measure provides data similar to previous data. *Intrareliability* refers to how consistently an individual fills out an outcome measure. *Interreliability* refers to how consistently more than one individual completes the assessment process. Means of determining reliability include the following techniques: test-retest, alternate forms, split-half or odd-even, and consistency between scales that measure the same phenomenon.

1. *Test-retest.* This tool uses a second administration of the assessment measure to the individual within a reasonable time period, usually a period of 1 to 2 weeks after the first administration. For example, a group of participants may be asked to complete a measure of anxiety symptoms on a Monday afternoon at a community-based health center. The same group is asked to take the measure again on a Monday afternoon in the same location 2 weeks later. Assuming the group has received no services related to anxiety, their scores should be similar for the measure at both points in time, given that the same participants are completing the measure under the same basic conditions. If the scores are different, this could indicate a problem with test-retest reliability. If the items on the measure are confusing, the group may respond differently at different points in time because they interpret the meaning of the questions differently.

2. *Alternate forms.* Two scales are created from a pool of items measuring some attribute, using random selection to determine on which scale an item will appear. If the items are consistent in the measurement of the attribute, then agreement between the scales should be good.

3. *Split-half or odd-even.* If an instrument is measuring the same attribute throughout the inventory, consistency should occur between the odd and even items or between the first half and last half of the scale items.

4. *Internal consistency.* Items within a measure should yield consistent results. Thus, if the items within a questionnaire are measuring the same construct, individuals completing the measure should respond consistently to each item within a scale.

5. *Interrater reliability.* When two or more raters complete a measure or conduct an observation of the same behavior, their ratings should be correlated so as to indicate some consensus about the behavior they are measuring.

One of the most useful examples of reliability is research on the *Diagnostic and Statistical Manual of Mental Disorders (DSM-IV)*, the most highly utilized practitioners' tool for diagnosis. Leventhal and Martell (2006) point out that the interrater reliability criterion selected for categories of behaviors, including depression, described in the *DSM-IV* is 0.7. In other words, the correlation, or agreement, between different individuals' judgments about whether to assign a diagnosis should be at least 0.7, which is generally considered to be minimally acceptable (a value of 1.0 would indicate perfect agreement among raters). However, only a limited number of categories (25%) met the 0.7 criterion. An alternative to the *DSM-IV* description of depression is to conceptualize depression in terms of behaviors, stimulus control of behavior, and reinforcement systems. In other words, what are the behaviors associated with the experience of depression, and how are those behaviors reinforced internally and in the client's environment?

Validity

It is essential to use instruments that are reliable because a measure must provide consistent data before it can be valid. If a measure is valid, the inventory measures what it purports to measure. Fewer reports of validity than of reliability occur in behavioral science. This severe deficiency may be due to the substantial time and energy required to execute various validations. Types of validity procedures include face, predictive, concurrent, content, convergent and discriminative, and construct.

1. *Face.* The clinician looks at an inventory and determines whether this scale contains items that reflect the phenomenon of interest. If a measure has face validity, it appears to be relevant for measuring a phenomenon based on the judgment of the clinician or researcher. For example, an inventory used to report delinquent behavior among youth should contain items relating to such activities as stealing, drinking, aggressive assaults, and drug usage.

2. *Predictive.* An instrument should be able to predict the future behavior of the individual. The use of grades, Graduate Record Examination scores, letters of reference, interviews, and Miller Analogies Test scores to help predict performance in graduate social work education are familiar examples. Similarly, if participants' scores on a depression screening indicate depressive symptoms and these participants are more likely to be later diagnosed with depression than those whose scores fall into the normal range, this will provide evidence of predictive validity. The ability to predict behavior based on historical factors is one challenge that faces the helping professions.

3. *Concurrent.* This procedure relates the scores of one assessment inventory with an inventory for which validity already has been established. Thus, if an inventory such as the Jesness Inventory (1969), which has an established reputation for tapping antisocial behavior, agrees with scores derived from a checklist measuring specific types of antisocial behavior, validity of the latter inventory may be inferred.

4. *Content.* An instrument should have enough items to adequately measure the phenomenon of interest. For example, content can be assessed in a measurement of antisocial behavior by asking whether enough items are contained in the instrument to measure the various aspects of the behavior, such as gross motor behaviors, physical contacts, verbalizations, throwing objects, or other distracting behaviors.

5. *Convergent and discriminative.* Tests that measure the same phenomenon should correlate; tests that do not measure the same phenomenon should not correlate. For example, no substantial differences should occur between results of the various classical measures of delinquency, such as the Jesness Inventory (1969), whereas results of such inventories should not correlate highly with scales measuring another phenomenon, such as anxiety.

6. *Construct.* A theoretical framework is chosen, and client behavior is predicted. If the predictions are accurate, the inventory is assumed to measure the attribute. For example, it is predicted that an individual diagnosed with an anxiety disorder experiences more symptoms of anxiety than those diagnosed with a psychotic disorder. If those diagnosed with an anxiety disorder score higher on a measure of anxiety than those with a psychotic disorder, this is evidence that the measure has construct validity.

ASSESSMENT PROCEDURES

The wide range of assessment procedures available for measuring behavior allows for choosing strategies that are empirically sound and appropriate for the needs of individual clients and the agency context. The following section describes a number of these procedures and draws on examples from a study conducted in St. Louis examining behavior of children within a community center who were identified as antisocial.

Behavioral Observation (Time Sampling): Clients

A nonparticipant observational technique may be used to measure the frequency of behavior exhibited by clients. This procedure is frequently implemented in social work practice. For the St. Louis study, behavioral observations were used to measure changes in behavior (Feldman, Caplinger, & Wodarski, 1983). The observers remained as unobtrusive as possible by avoiding virtually all social interactions with the group. The children were informed that the observers would not interfere with the group in any way, that all the information obtained would be confidential and would be reviewed only by the research team, and that they could help the observers do their job by ignoring them as much as possible.

A checklist that yielded highly reliable data was used to tabulate the incidence of prosocial, nonsocial, and antisocial behaviors observed. Checklist reliability was established through simultaneous ratings of behavior recorded on videotapes illustrating the small-group behavior of similar children. The tapes included numerous illustrations of antisocial behavior. Observers also were trained using these videotapes. The training sessions were completed when each observer could reliably agree on behavioral coding with one of the investigators and the other observers at a level of 0.99 or above, utilizing the rating categories described in Appendix A of this chapter. Observations were made every 10 seconds in a fixed order, for one of the children, then for another child, and so on until all the children had been observed. The procedure was repeated for the duration of the group meeting or group activities at the summer camp. To minimize bias due to the observers' expectations, observers were not informed of the hypothesized changes for each experimental condition or any particular subject.

To ensure consistent agreement among the observers during the 3-year study, 189 separate reliability checks were performed on the ratings at the community center and the summer camp. These checks were made by having the observers simultaneously rate the interaction of children on videotapes. Different tapes illustrating children interacting in various types of situations, such as discussing difficulties (e.g., at school and with parents, drugs, sex, girls, or boys), painting, playing ball, or building a campfire, were used in each reliability session to prevent the observers from rating a child solely on the basis of previous acquaintance with the videotape. The tapes included numerous illustrations of antisocial behavior. The following formula yielded a ratio of interobserver agreement, interval by interval: number of agreements/(number of agreements + number of disagreements). Observers were required to have a reliability rating consistently above 0.090.

To systematize observers' ratings, a recording scheme was devised based on the assessment of three types of subject behaviors; observer ratings were based solely on those three behavioral categories. (See Appendix A for instructions on administration of the scale and definitions of behavioral categories.)

Strengths

- Provides highly reliable data; research indicates that behavior time sampling represents actual frequencies of behavior (Bloom et al., 2009)

- Permits comparison of individuals and group data

- Provides a large amount of longitudinal data to enable assessment of change over time

Weaknesses

- Securing data is costly in financial assets, energy of the researchers, and administrative constraints

- Data limited to a specific context

- All behaviors are equally rated

- Possibility that some behaviors may not have been included in the definition or occurred so infrequently as not to have been observed

Behavioral Observations (Time Sampling): Practitioners

Observers rated the behaviors of the practitioners in the community center as well as those of the children. After rating the behaviors of all the children in the group, the observer then rated the behavior of the practitioner before proceeding to rate the children again. This procedure produced 60 to 120 observations of practitioner behavior per session (sessions were 2 hours). Financial and administrative concerns permitted this type of sampling procedure only infrequently. The ideal situation would have been to observe the practitioner after each observation of a child. Such a process would enable direct isolation of the effects of practitioner behavior on the child. Reliability for this part of the checklist was established in the same manner as described for the other part of the checklist. The training sessions were completed when each observer could agree with the others at a level of 0.85 or above, utilizing the rating categories to be described shortly. This criterion was considered adequate because the various behaviors could be scored into 18 categories. To ensure consistent agreement among the observers, 189 separate reliability checks were performed.

The observers rated a practitioner's behavior according to the general category of whether the practitioner intervened on an individual level (i.e., directed individual interventions toward a certain child with the specific purpose of increasing, decreasing, stopping, or maintaining behaviors that child exhibited), or on a group level (i.e., performed group interventions toward two or more children with the specific purpose of increasing, decreasing, stopping, or maintaining behaviors exhibited by those children). The observer then specified the practitioner's behavior with respect to the following categories: directions, physical contact, praise, positive attention, holding, criticism, threats, negative attention, and time-out. (See Appendix A for instructions on administration of the scale and definition of leader behavior categories.)

Strengths

- Provides highly reliable data

- Provides data that indicate whether treatment was implemented

- Permits comparison of a child's behavioral change over time with practitioner interventions

Weakness

- Categories may not be relevant to the assessment of whether treatment was implemented; that is, other categories may be more appropriate to test whether treatment was implemented

Inventory Assessment of Type of Treatment and Its Implementation by Practitioners

Following each meeting, observers filled out a scale indicating the type of treatment method employed. (See Appendix A for instructions on administration of the scale and definition of treatment methods.)

Strength

- Provides an additional source of data on the implementation of treatment

Weakness

- Characteristically, reliability checks are not executed on these types of data, as was the case in this study

Self-Inventories Completed by Children

For the same study described above, all children completed two types of self-inventories at the community center. The inventories were administered 8 weeks after the initial session of the program and 4 weeks before the program terminated. Approximately 5 months elapsed between the test periods. The first inventory, titled "Child's Checklist," was designed to measure the average incidence of prosocial, nonsocial, and antisocial behaviors that a child thinks he or she exhibits during an average week. Behaviors listed on the checklist were analogous to the behavior contained within the behavior time-sampling method. At the same time, a similar inventory, titled "Therapist's Checklist," was administered to the children's group practitioners. In addition, the children also completed a subclass of the Jesness Inventory (1969), designed to measure self-reported tendencies toward manifest aggression. The manifest aggression scale consists of 31 items. Jesness contends that these items reflect an awareness of unpleasant feelings, especially of anger and frustration, a tendency to react readily with these emotions, and other obvious discomfort concerning the presence and control of these feelings. (See Appendix C for the Child's Checklist.)

Strengths

- Measures perceptual attributes that behavioral measurements do not tap

- Requires less financial cost, time, and energy; entails fewer organizational and administrative constraints

- Enables the comparison of data provided in the study with those of other studies

Weaknesses

- Low reliability between measures that purport to measure the same item

- When tests are limited to pre- and posttests, power to assess change over time is reduced

- Younger children may not interpret questions correctly, and in some instances, do not understand the instructions

Inventories Completed by Other Significant Adults in Child's Life

The checklist used for the St. Louis study is analogous to the inventories filled out by children except that it is completed by a referral agent, a parent, group leaders, or behavioral observers. Behaviors denoted on the checklist were similar to those listed on an observational scale used for the research and those reported on a self-inventory completed by the children. (See Appendix D for the Observer's Checklist.)

Strengths

- Provides data from significant adults on how they perceive the effects of the program
- Provides data on child's behavior outside the treatment context

Weaknesses

- Low correlations between significant others' ratings of child's behavior
- Lack of uniformity in filling out the inventory

Interviewing Schedules Completed by Parents

Interview schedules typically include open-ended questions and allow the respondents to provide richer detail about their experiences. The schedules used for the St. Louis study introduced parents to the program and helped secure necessary background data. They also provide an opportunity for answering questions parents have about programs. (See Appendix E for the interview schedule.)

Strengths

- Provides additional sources of information
- Enables more flexibility in securing the information
- Provides opportunity to clarify questions
- Helps participant become familiar with treatment context

Weaknesses

- Difficulty in analyzing data—that is, how it relates to empirical questions
- Problems in controlling how consistently the interview is conducted
- Costly in terms of money and time

CHOICE OF MEASURES

The decision concerning which of the various types of measures should be used rests on the aims of the empirical evaluation. Both self-inventories and behavior scales have certain advantages and obvious drawbacks. Self-inventories have low reliability, but they cost less; also, they may measure behavioral tendencies that behavioral scales do not measure. Self-inventories such as individualized rating scales and client logs can also be tailored specifically to each client so they will be highly relevant for the presenting problem, as conceptualized by the client (Bloom et al., 2009). Behavioral scales provide highly reliable data but are more costly and, depending on the breadth of observation, may provide data limited to a specific social context. The most direct measure of client behavior is behavioral observation, and this is a highly reliable and valid measurement strategy when observers are well trained. If an appropriate behavioral observation scale is not available, then investigators can develop their own scale by observing clients systematically and then defining the relevant behaviors in such a way that two people can consistently agree these behaviors have occurred.

When using questionnaires and interview schedules, it is important to know whether they have been pretested with a similar client population. For example, before administering a measure of depressive symptoms with a male, Latino client, it is important to know whether this measure has been used successfully with other male, Latino clients in the past. If the measure has been used with this population and has demonstrated good reliability and validity, the worker can be more confident that the measure will be appropriate for his or her client. Even when a measure has been explicitly tested with a particular client population, it is often helpful to pretest a measure by administering it to a few members of that population to determine whether they find it to be understandable, feasible, and relevant for them (Rubin & Babbie, 2007).

Interview schedules are excellent devices in beginning empirical evaluation when research questions are not clearly formulated, because they typically include open-ended questions that provide an opportunity for clients to give in-depth answers that may help the evaluator refine research questions and hypotheses. Interview schedules should be constructed with the rationale for collection clearly resolved by the empirical researchers. Questions for interviews and questionnaires should be stated in a manner that facilitates the ease of responses and requires little interpretation by the clients. Brief questions that address a single issue are easier for clients to interpret. By contrast, double-barreled questions that ask about two issues at the same time can lead to confusion and inconsistent responses across clients. For example, the following question is confusing because it asks a student to report about multiple issues simultaneously: How much support do you receive from teachers and your principal? This question also may be unclear because students may interpret the meaning of "support" differently. A less confusing method would be to ask whether students agree or disagree with a statement such as "My teachers care whether or not I come to school," and then to include a separate question about whether the principal cares that they come to school. This question could be combined with an open-ended question—such as "Why?"—so students could elaborate on their reasons for agreeing or disagreeing with the statement. Questionnaires and interviews should be brief to prevent fatigue for the investigator and client.

SINGLE-CRITERION VERSUS MULTICRITERIA MEASUREMENT

Although studies often use single-criterion measures of behavior change, this can be problematic, since a single criterion is not likely to capture the many possible dimensions of change in human behavior. An example of a single-criterion measure is a self-report measure of substance use behaviors or depressive symptoms. These measures, used in isolation, are limited in that they provide the data from only one person's perspective. These self-report measures also tend to assess for a targeted behavior rather than for multiple, interrelated behaviors and processes, such as interactions with others in the person's environment.

Multicriteria measurements, on the other hand, tap a wider range of possible avenues of change; for this reason, many researchers over the past decade have encouraged using them to evaluate therapeutic services to maximize the possibility of capturing change in the various dimensions of human behavior. For example, in multicriteria measurements, self-assessment, assessments by others, and behavior observations could be used concurrently for a more comprehensive evaluation of client change (Thyer & Wodarski, 2007). Multicriteria measures of behavior, such as the Achenbach Child Behavior Checklist, assess for a range of internalizing and externalizing behaviors and measure the behavior from the perspectives of youths, teachers, and parents. This type of measure allows for assessing multiple dimensions of behavior and obtaining this information from multiple perspectives.

Multicriteria measures are helpful when they use different types of measurement strategies that have different strengths and limitations. A self-report measure, for example, may be vulnerable to social desirability bias. Data from a self-report measure may be supplemented with data from direct behavioral observation to provide the practitioner with a more accurate account of the client's behavior. If the data point to similar behavioral issues, the practitioner can be more confident that the behavior is being measured accurately. If the two types of measure diverge, the practitioner may conclude that one or both of the measures are limited in their ability to accurately assess the client's behavior.

Indeed, it is often the case that different measures of the same behavior correlate poorly with each other (Jastrowski Mano, Davies, Klein-Tasman, & Adesso, 2009; Konold, Walthall, & Pianta, 2004; Wodarski & Bagarozzi, 1979). For example, ratings of children's behavior by teachers, parents, and the children themselves often diverge. Recent research suggests that these differing reports may be due to the fact that children's behavior is likely to be variable across different contexts, such as school and home (Konold et al., 2004). That multiple measures of the same behavior often correlate poorly with one another further emphasizes the importance of using more than one measure in order to obtain an understanding of behavior from multiple perspectives. Integrating these different sources of information will require that clinicians use critical thinking skills in weighing different sources of evidence.

Consumer assessment of benefits should be considered in the evaluation of outcomes even though such an assessment is a difficult methodological issue to resolve when outcomes differ from the criteria established by research (Wodarski, 1981). In our case, consumer evaluation of two community-based treatment programs for children with antisocial behaviors was favorable. Similar responses are reflected in data obtained from parents' evaluation of both community-based treatment programs for predelinquent and delinquent children (Wodarski, 1981). In both cases, however, consumer assessments were not compatible with other data, indicating that the consumer may use different criteria for evaluation than researchers do.

ADEQUATE SPECIFICATION OF BEHAVIOR AND BASELINES

An adequate treatment program must consider the need for reliable specification of target behaviors that are to be changed by whatever means used to measure them—such as questionnaires, interviews, or behavioral observations. For example, a treatment program to alleviate antisocial behavior might employ behavioral rating scales in which the deviant behaviors are highly specified. These could include such observable behaviors as hitting others, damaging physical property, running away, throwing objects, climbing and jumping out windows, and making loud noises and aggressive or threatening verbal statements.

Whatever the mode of measurement, for the adequate evaluation of any therapeutic service, the investigator must secure a baseline before implementing treatment. A baseline measurement provides a record of the state of the presenting problem before an intervention is provided. Subsequent measurement data can be compared with the baseline data to determine whether clients have improved in targeted areas. This baseline can also enable the investigator to assess how the treatment interventions compare with no treatment interventions. Behavioral observations are less susceptible to observer bias if observers are trained to record specific behavior and are unaware of the research questions and researcher's predictions related to client outcomes. Observers may be trained, as they were for the St. Louis study described earlier, by conducting observations of videotaped behavior prior to observations of actual behaviors for the study. By comparing the ratings across observers, the researcher can identify whether there are inconsistencies in ratings and provide more guidance to observers in how behaviors are to be recorded.

When it is not feasible to employ trained observers, a baseline may be recorded by the client or by significant others in his or her environment. These baselines, although less reliable, are often necessary because of various organizational or other environmental constraints. Some of these constraints may be lack of money for trained observers or behaviors that occur at times when they are not readily observable by others. When the practitioner uses baseline data not secured by a trained observer, the data should be obtained from two or more independent sources in order to check consistency. For example, a family may be asked to record the number of positive interactions among family members during dinnertime each evening for 2 weeks prior to beginning an intervention aimed at improving family communication. A parent and a child may be asked to keep separate logs of positive interactions so these different sources can be compared in understanding the quality of family communication before the intervention. Ratings of positive interactions can be tracked during the course of the intervention and compared with the baseline ratings to determine whether positive interactions occur more frequently over time.

The following are considerations that should be addressed before a practitioner decides on the exact procedure for securing a baseline. First, context in which the individual's target behavior occurs at a high frequency should be chosen. If the behavior occurs in more than one context, baselines may be secured for each context if possible. Such a procedure enables the assessment of a broader range of contexts in which the behavior occurs, contributes to the determination of whether behavioral changes in one context are analogous to those changes in another context, and provides a more accurate measure of behavior (Wodarski, 1997). Another consideration is the accessibility of the behavior. If the behavior is readily observable, this will not be a problem. If it is inaccessible, such as a behavior that occurs late at night or in contexts where observation is not possible, the investigator must use reports by the clients or others present when the behavior occurs to secure the data.

Overview

This chapter emphasizes the importance of choosing outcome criteria for research and reviews basic considerations for choosing appropriate outcome measures. Following the choice of types of measures, adequate baseline rates must be secured. Another essential prerequisite of empirical research is the assessment of the reliability and validity of the means to secure data. A researcher must address certain questions regarding the data in order to evaluate a program. The means available to collect the data must be decided based on the strengths and weaknesses of the measure. As research and practice become more integrated, practitioners should include such considerations in their treatment plans, which will ultimately improve services offered to clients. Moreover, more sophisticated research should include short-term outcomes and long-term outcomes.

Questions for Discussion

1. A teacher refers a child to the school social worker for escalating incidents of disruptive behavior in the classroom. Behaviors include interrupting the teacher and other students, taking materials away from other students, yelling in the classroom, and hitting other students.

    a. Create a question that will guide your practice with this client and help you evaluate the effectiveness of your work.
    b. How would you measure your effectiveness with this client in a way that would help you answer your practice question and make a good judgment about the effectiveness of your intervention(s)?
    c. What are the strengths and limitations of the measure(s) you identified above?
    d. How would you assess the client's perspective about the measure(s) you identified?
    e. How would you proceed if the client expressed discomfort with a particular measurement strategy?

References

Bloom, M., Fischer, J., & Orme, J. G. (2009). *Evaluating practice: Guidelines for the accountable professional* (6th ed.). Boston: Allyn & Bacon.

Feldman, R. A., Caplinger, T. E., & Wodarski, J. S. (1983). *The St. Louis conundrum: The effective treatment of antisocial youths.* Englewood Cliffs, NJ: Prentice Hall.

Fischer, J., & Corcoran, K. (2007). *Measures for clinical practice and research* (Vols. 1–2). New York: Oxford University Press.

Jastrowski Mano, K., Davies, H. W., Klein-Tasman, B., & Adesso, V. (2009). Measurement equivalence of the child behavior checklist among parents of African American adolescents. *Journal of Child and Family Studies, 18*(5), 606–620.

Jesness, C. F. (1969). *The Jesness Inventory manual.* Palo Alto, CA: Consulting Psychologist Press.

Konold, T. R., Walthall, J. C., & Pianta, R. C. (2004). The behavior of child behavior ratings: Measurement structure of the child behavior checklist across time, informants, and child gender. *Behavioral Disorders, 29*(4), 372–383.

Leventhal, A., & Martell, C. (2006). *The myth of depression as disease: Limitations and alternatives to drugs.* Westport, CT: Praeger.

Rubin, A., & Babbie, E. (2007). *Research methods for social work* (6th ed.). Belmont, CA: Brooks Cole.

Thyer, B. A., & Wodarski, J. S. (Eds.). (2007). *Social work in mental health: An evidence-based approach.* Hoboken, NJ: Wiley.

Wodarski, J. S. (1981). Group work with antisocial children. In S. P. Schinke (Ed.), *Community application of behavioral methods: A sourcebook for social workers.* Chicago: Aldine.

Wodarski, J. S. (1997). *Research methods for clinical social workers.* New York: Springer.

Wodarski, J. S., & Bagarozzi, D. (1979). *Behavioral social work: An introduction.* New York: Human Sciences Press.

Wodarski, J. S., & Feit, M. D. (2009). *Evidence-based intervention in social work: A practitioner's manual.* Springfield, IL: Charles C Thomas.

Appendix A: Instructions for Administration of the Checklists

Observations are made at 10-second intervals. Observe the child at the beginning of the 10-second interval, and record on the checklist the first behavior exhibited. After all children are observed once, please mark the leader's behavior by observing him or her at the beginning of the 10-second interval and by recording on the rating scale the first behavior exhibited (Figure A.1). Repeat this procedure throughout the observational period. Circle the data box on the checklist when the group activity changes. Indicate what the previous activity was on the blank line at the end of the first data row, or what the new activity is on the line at the end of the second data row. Repeat this procedure as necessary.

The numbers 1, 2, and 3 stand, respectively, for the ratings of prosocial, nonsocial, and antisocial behaviors.

PROSOCIAL BEHAVIOR

Mark "1" if the child exhibits any of the following behaviors:

1. One child hands another child a material object, such as a basketball or hockey stick, which the latter child needs to continue participating in the group activity.

2. One child asks the group leader or another child to help someone in the activity.

3. Two children work on the same activity together. For example, one child shows the other how or helps the other child overcome difficulties so they may execute the activity.

4. One child helps another participate in the discussion of some topic by making a comment that elicits continued verbal behavior. Example: One child is talking about drugs, and the other says "good point," "please continue," or "tell us more."

5. A child engages in the group activity.

6. A child asks the worker about the group activity.

7. A child engages in the decision-making process verbally or nonverbally: for example, nods his head, pats another child for engaging in the process, smiles, is listening or sitting, makes eye contact with the worker or another child.

FIGURE A.1 Rating Scale

DATE_____ OBSERVER_____ GROUP_____

NAME ACTIVITY

	123	123	123	123	123	123	123	123	123	123
	123	123	123	123	123	123	123	123	123	123
	123	123	123	123	123	123	123	123	123	123
	123	123	123	123	123	123	123	123	123	123
	123	123	123	123	123	123	123	123	123	123
	123	123	123	123	123	123	123	123	123	123
	123	123	123	123	123	123	123	123	123	123
	123	123	123	123	123	123	123	123	123	123
	123	123	123	123	123	123	123	123	123	123
	123	123	123	123	123	123	123	123	123	123
	123	123	123	123	123	123	123	123	123	123
	D H	D H	D H	D H	D H	D H	D H	D H	D H	D H
	PC C	PC C	PC C	PC C	PC C	PC C	PC C	PC C	PC C	PC C
	P T	P T	P T	P T	P T	P T	P T	P T	P T	P T
	PA NA	PA NA	PA NA	PA NA	PA NA	PA NA	PA NA	PA NA	PA NA	PA NA
	TO	TO	TO	TO	TO	TO	TO	TO	TO	TO

8. A child makes an appropriate comment.

9. A child tries to help someone, shares something with another child, stops other children from arguing or fighting, helps children be friends with one another, or tries to do something nice even though nobody expected it.

10. A child says nice things to another child, such as "I like you."

11. A child helps other group members straighten up their belongings, solve a problem, or fix something that was broken.

12. A child helps the group leader by paying attention, cooperating, or carrying out the leader's reasonable instructions.

NONSOCIAL BEHAVIOR

Mark "2" if the child you observe exhibits any of the following nonparticipating behaviors:

1. The child looks out the window or stares into space.

2. The child plays with some object but does not disturb other children.

3. The child does not engage in appropriate tasks for the interactional situation: for example, the children are playing basketball, but he or she sits in the corner.

4. The child lays his or her head on the table or furniture.

5. The child pulls at his or her hair or clothing.

6. The child cleans or digs in the desk or table without disturbing another pupil.

7. The child draws on the desk or table.

8. The child plays with a wallet, purse, or book.

9. The child sucks his or her thumb or other objects.

10. The child bites his or her nails.

11. The child engages in motor activities that do not disturb others: for example, takes off his or her shoes, rocks in a chair, moves a chair in place, or sits out of position.

ANTISOCIAL BEHAVIOR

Mark "3" if the child you observed exhibits any of the following behaviors:

1. *Verbalizations.* The child talks to another child and, thus, disrupts the other child's participation in the group activity; the child talks to another child and, thus, disrupts someone else who is trying to participate in the group activity; the child speaks without directing the conversation toward anyone; the child engages in name calling, crying, screaming, laughing loudly, coughing loudly, singing disruptively, or whistling disruptively.

2. *Gross motor behaviors.* If the children are seated around the table, the child is out of his or her seat without the group worker's permission running, jumping, skipping, standing up, hopping, moving a chair, or walking around, which disrupts the group activities.

3. *Object interference.* A child plays with some object that interferes with another child's participating in the group: for example, taps a pencil or other object, claps, taps feet, rattles or tears paper, throws books on table, or slams things on furniture.

4. *Physical contacts.* Contact is initiated by one child toward another who is participating in the group activity. This contact disrupts the latter child's participation. The contact may include hitting, kicking, shoving, pinching, slapping, striking with an object, throwing an object that hits another person, poking with an object, biting, pulling hair, touching, patting, or disturbing another child's property.

5. *Distracting behaviors.* A child engages in physical movement that attracts another child's attention and causes that child to stop participation in the group activity. The first child may turn his or her head or body to look at another child, show an object to another child, rock in a chair, sit out of position, or rummage in furniture.

TYPE OF INTERVENTION

If the group worker is not intervening at the time you observe him or her, just leave these letters blank. If the group worker has intervened, specify whether he or she intervened on a group level (G) or on an individual level (I).

1. Please mark "I" if the group worker exhibited any of the following individual interventions toward one certain child with the specific purpose of increasing, decreasing, stopping, or maintaining behaviors the child exhibits: physical contact, praise, facial expression, attention, holding, suggestion, criticism, threat, negative attention, time-out.

2. Please mark "G" if the worker exhibited any of the following group interventions toward two or more children with the specific purpose of increasing, decreasing, stopping, or maintaining behaviors exhibited by two or more children: physical contact, praise, facial expression, attention, suggestion, criticism, threats, negative attention, time-out.

WORKER'S BEHAVIOR

Please mark the appropriate letter that corresponds to the worker's behavior that you observed.

Positive Reinforcement

Directions (comments that request group members to exhibit a specific behavior)

1. Therapist asks children to clean up materials.

2. Therapist suggests alternate activity for the group: for example, by saying "Let's go to the gym" or "Let's start on our models."

Physical contact (positive contact between the group leader and the child)

1. Embraces the child while the child is in an activity

2. Pats the child while the child is in an activity

3. Holds the child's arm or hand while the child is in an activity

Praise (comments that indicate approval, commendation, or achievement)

1. Says "That was good" to a child who is participating

2. Says "You are doing it right" to a child who is participating

3. Says "You are studying well" to a child who is participating

4. Says "I like you" to a child who is participating

5. Says "You made me happy" to a child who is participating

Note: Facial expressions of the worker are considered a positive intervention if the group leader smiles or nods to the child while the child is participating in an activity.

Positive attention is also considered a positive intervention if the group leader directs it toward a certain child while the child is participating in an activity.

Punishing Interventions

Holding (the group leader's physical grasping of the child)

1. Forcibly holding the child

2. Putting the child in the hall

3. Grabbing the child

Criticism (from the group leader)

1. Yelling

2. Scolding

3. Raising voice and using such statements as "Don't do that!" "Be quiet!" "Sit in your place!" "That's wrong!" "Stop talking!" "Did I call on you?" "Are you wasting time?" "Don't laugh!" "You know what you are supposed to do!"

Note: Threats (the group leader's statement of undesired consequences to occur at a later time). Examples: "If you aren't quiet, we won't go to the gym." "If you don't stop fighting, we won't take the ride on the bus." "No ice cream for you guys until you clean up!"

Negative attention (the group leader frowns or grimaces at the child)

Time-out refers to specific disciplinary procedures wherein the child is removed from the activity, thus depriving the child of obtaining reinforcement or participating in the group activity.

TREATMENT METHOD

This inventory will be filled out at the end of each group meeting. It will be the last data sheet in the packet.

Check the blank that best describes the treatment method the leader used during most of the meeting: _____ social learning _____ traditional _____ group-centered _____ none

If the leader used other treatment methods in addition to the one mentioned above, but not for most of the meeting, please check the blank that corresponds to the treatment methods utilized: _____ social learning _____ traditional _____ group-centered _____ none

Note: If one child initiates an antisocial behavior and that behavior is emulated by another child when the latter's observational period occurs, the behavior of the latter child is coded as antisocial.

If a child leaves the group because of anger or frustration, you do not record data (such as "3") for that child while he or she is out of the room.

COMMENCEMENT OF DATA COLLECTION

Begin 5 minutes before the official starting time for the group meeting. If the leader is present, star the first box on your data sheet. If the leader is not present, star the appropriate data box when he or she joins the group. This same procedure is to be used whenever the leader departs from the meeting (use a triangle to denote return).

GOING FROM ACTIVITY TO ACTIVITY

No data will be taken while a group is in transit, either within the building or outside the building. An empty box on the data sheet will designate that the child was not present at that moment; nevertheless, a 10-second period should elapse before the next child is observed. This procedure should be followed throughout the meeting. If certain children are absent from the meeting, 10-second intervals should elapse for every child absent before the next child is observed. This procedure also should be followed throughout the meeting.

GROUP SPLITTING

The observer will take data even if some of the children leave the group. The observer should continue to record for that portion of the group that has the leader present, regardless of the physical context (i.e., club room, gym). This procedure also should be followed in contexts other than the treatment center. Skip the appropriate time intervals for children who are not present. A blank data box indicates that the child has left the group. Leave his or her data boxes blank until he or she returns, then begin securing data again at the appropriate time interval.

IDENTIFICATION OF CHILDREN

1. At the first meeting, you and the children will be introduced to one another. Try to identify the children by certain outstanding characteristics so you can record behavior.

2. After the meeting, check with the worker so you can match the child's characteristics with the child's name.

AMBIGUOUS BEHAVIORS

You must record each observed behavior for a child as "1," "2," or "3." However, if certain types of coding responses are questionable or in doubt, seek clarification from the project directors after the meeting.

Appendix B: Observer's Report

Date:

Group:

Leader:

Observer:

Indicate the basic leadership style used (1, 2, or 3):

1. The leader seldom, if ever, structured group activities, friendship relationships, and task relationships. The leader permitted members to select their own activities and develop their own friendship, task, and interpersonal relationships with one another.

2. The leader structured group activities, friendship relationships, and task relationships by helping members set specific group goals with specific ensuing rewards for the group as a whole or for individual members. Usually, all members were expected to share equally in the rewards, if any, of the group's goal-attainment endeavors.

3. The leader structured group activities, friendship relationships, and task relationships by helping both the individual members and the group as a whole set goals. Without delineating specific rewards, selected individual members were expected to engage in certain relationships, thus benefiting from them, and the group as a whole sometimes was expected to benefit from certain group-oriented interventions by the leader.

Appendix C: Child's Checklist

Name:

Group:

Date:

Directions: The research staff asks that you answer the following questions voluntarily. We think you will enjoy this. It is not a test like reading or arithmetic. There is no grade or mark. When we ask you about things, the only right answer is exactly what you honestly tell us. Each of you may give a different answer, and all of you will still be right. For example, if we ask, "How many ice cream cones did you eat yesterday?" each of you could say a different number, and all of you will be giving the right answer.

Your answers will be seen only by the research staff. No one else will ever see your answers. That includes the group leader, supervisory staff, your parents, your friends, or anyone else. Be completely honest in your answers.

OK, let's go! Please tell us the number of times you think you did these things during the past week. Don't include those that were done accidentally.

1. _____ How many times did you say nice things, such as "I like you," to someone?

2. _____ How many times did you help your friends by paying attention to them, cooperating with them, or staying with them until you both finished what you started out to do?

3. _____ How many times did you help adults by paying attention to them, cooperating with them, staying with them until you both finished what you started out to do, or by carrying out reasonable requests or instructions?

4. _____ How many times did you try to help someone, share something of yours, stop others from arguing or fighting, help other boys or girls be friends with one another, or try to do something nice even though nobody expected it?

5. _____ How many times did you bother adults by being restless, moving about, tapping an object, having a temper tantrum, or not carrying out reasonable requests or instructions?

6. _____ How many times did you destroy, break, or mess up someone else's things?

7. _____ How many times did you hit, kick, shove, bite, pinch, slap, pull someone's hair, hit someone with an object, or throw an object?

8.   _____ How many times did you help someone straighten up his or her belongings, solve a problem, or fix something that was broken?

9.   _____ How many times did you take something that was not yours?

10.   _____ How many times did you bother your friends by being restless, moving about, tapping an object, or having a temper tantrum?

11.   _____ How many times did you say bad things, such as "I'll kill you," to someone? Do not include swearing.

12.   _____ How many times did you help someone get back a thing that was lost or missing?

13.   _____ How many times did you act like a "loner" when with a group of friends or adults? That is, how many times did you play alone, stare out the window, fall asleep, or do other things like that?

Thank you for answering these questions.

Appendix D: Observer's Checklist

Child:

Group:

Date:

Observer:

Directions: Please answer the following questions for the child listed above. Your answers will be seen only by the research staff and will not be communicated to supervisory staff, parents, or anyone else other than research staff.

Please tell us the numbers of times you think the child did these things during the past week. Don't include those that were done accidentally.

1. _____ How many times did he or she say nice things, such as "I like you," to someone?

2. _____ How many times did he or she help friends by paying attention to them, cooperating with them, or staying with them until they both finished what they started out to do?

3. _____ How many times did he or she help adults by paying attention to them, cooperating with them, staying with them until they both finished what they started out to do, or by carrying out reasonable requests or instructions?

4. _____ How many times did he or she try to help someone, share something of his or hers, stop other from arguing or fighting, help other boys or girls be friends with one another, or try to do something nice even though nobody expected it?

5. _____ How many times did he or she bother adults by being restless, moving about, tapping an object, having a temper tantrum, or not carrying out reasonable request or instructions?

6. _____ How many times did he or she destroy, break, or mess up someone else's things?

7. _____ How many times did he or she hit, kick, shove, bite, pinch, slap, pull someone's hair, hit someone with an object, or throw an object?

8. _____ How many times did he or she help someone straighten up his or her belongings, solve a problem, or fix something that was broken?

9. _____ How many times did he or she take something that was not his or hers?

10. _____ How many times did he or she bother friends by being restless, moving about, tapping an object, or having a temper tantrum?

11. _____ How many times did he or she say bad things, such as "I'll kill you," to someone? Do not include swearing.

12. _____ How many times did he or she help someone get back a thing that was lost or missing?

13. _____ How many times did he or she act like a "loner" when with a group of friends or adults? That is, how many times did he or she play alone, stare out the window, fall asleep, and do other things like that?

Thank you for answering these questions.

Appendix E: Intake Interview Schedule

I. PURPOSE OF THE PROGRAM

Our purpose is to help children who are having difficulty in relations with adults and/or children. We would like to enroll your child in one of the friendship groups the center provides. These groups engage in different activities that may improve how your child gets along with children and adults. In the past, these groups have helped children with various types of social and behavioral problems.

II. OVERVIEW OF THIS INTERVIEW

A. I will go into more detail regarding the program.

B. I will ask you a variety of questions that will help us determine whether your child can be included in the program. (Any and all information will be confidential.)

C. We will discuss the financing of your child's activity at the community center.

D. We will discuss government requirements, since our program is financed through a federal research grant.

E. We will try to determine periods when your child has free time in order to help us find a convenient group for him or her.

F. If you would like, we will tour the facilities of the center.

III. FURTHER EXPLANATION OF THE PROGRAM

A. The group will be a regular friendship or activity group at the community center.

1. These groups usually engage in a variety of activities, such as basketball, swimming, handball, and participation in community projects.
2. Most groups will have 8 to 12 members.

B. The groups generally meet for 2 hours a week, usually during a weekday after school or on the weekend. The groups will meet for about 15 weeks.

C. The meetings will usually be held in _____. If your child is accepted for the program, he or she will receive a letter or telephone call from a staff member to notify him or her of the time and place for the first meeting. Meetings will begin around _____.

D. Group leaders will be either regular community center group leaders (usually college students interested in working with children) or graduate students at a graduate school of social work. All group leaders

1. have had previous experience working with children's groups,
2. have undergone special training for this program, and
3. will be under the supervision of a professional staff member.

IV. SCHEDULING

Which of the following times could your child attend a club meeting? Indicate by placing an X in the appropriate box.

	Sun	Mon	Tue	Wed	Thur	Fri	Sat
1 PM							
2 PM							
3 PM							
4 PM							
5 PM							
6 PM							
7 PM							
8 PM							
9 PM							

V. BACKGROUND DATA

Now, we would like to ask a number of routine questions for the program. As with all other information you give me, your answers will be confidential.

Please answer the following questions.

A. Information concerning father

1. Age:
2. Religion:
3. Occupation:

4. Gross yearly income (check one):

   None
   $1,000–$3,000
   $3,001–$6,000
   $6,001–$9,000
   $9,001–$12,000
   $12,001–$15,000
   $15,001–$18,000
   $18,001–$21,000
   $21,001–$24,000
   $24,001 or above

5. Last year of school completed:

B. Information concerning mother

   1. Age:
   2. Religion:
   3. Occupation:
   4. Gross yearly income (check one):

      None
      $1,000–$3,000
      $3,001–$6,000
      $6,001–$9,000
      $9,001–$12,000
      $12,001–$15,000
      $15,001–$18,000
      $18,001–$21,000
      $21,001–$44,000
      $24,001 or above

   5. Last year of school completed:

C. Information concerning the child

   1. Current medical information:

      Please list any type of physical handicaps, medical information, or any other information the program staff should know about.

   2. Does the child's physical condition limit the child in any way with reference to participation in center activities?

      _____ Yes
      _____ No
      If yes, please describe.

      _____
      _____
      _____

3. What is your child's average school grade?

    _____

4. How much does your child like his or her present school?

    _____ Likes very much
    _____ Likes somewhat
    _____ Neither likes nor dislikes
    _____ Dislikes somewhat
    _____ Dislikes very much

5. Does your child have any particular learning difficulties?

    _____ Yes
    _____ No

If yes, please describe and indicate whether the child has been referred for special help.

_____

_____

_____

6. Is your child a foster child or adopted child?

    _____ Yes
    _____ No

7. Are there other children in the family?

    _____ Yes
    _____ No

If yes, list their names, sexes, and ages.

_____

_____

_____

8. Do any of the sisters or brothers (if applicable) have any particular learning difficulties?

    _____ Yes
    _____ No

9. Do any of the sisters or brothers (if any) have any particular behavioral difficulties?

    _____ Yes
    _____ No

If yes, please list child's name and indicate whether the child has been referred for special help.

_____

_____

_____

VI. DEVELOPMENTAL HISTORY

A. Behavioral difficulties

   1. At what age did his or her difficulties first start?

   2. Since they first started, have his or her difficulties (check one)

       _____ become worse?
       _____ become better?
       _____ remained about the same?

   3. Were there any outstanding events that occurred before the onset of his or her difficulties?

       _____ Yes
       _____ No

       If yes, describe the events and how long before the onset.

       _____
       _____
       _____

   4. Have there been any outstanding events that further contributed to these difficulties since they first started?

       _____ Yes
       _____ No

       If yes, describe the events.

       _____
       _____
       _____

   5. Whenever the difficulty occurs, are there other children or adults who seem to make it worse?

       _____ Yes
       _____ No

       If yes, please describe.

       _____
       _____
       _____

B. Pick three of the child's most serious difficulties (if there are three), and please answer the following questions concerning them.

   1. Difficulty 1

      a. Briefly describe the difficulty.

      _____
      _____
      _____

b. About how many times per week does it occur?

c. About how long does each incident last?

d. Describe what happens *just before* the difficulty occurs.

_____

_____

_____

e. Describe what happens *just after* the difficulty occurs.

_____

_____

_____

2. Difficulty 2

a. Briefly describe the difficulty.

_____

_____

_____

b. About how many times per week does it occur?

c. About how long does each incident last?

d. Describe what happens *just before* the difficulty occurs?

_____

_____

_____

e. Describe what happens *just after* the difficulty occurs.

_____

_____

_____

3. Difficulty 3

a. Briefly describe the difficulty.

_____

_____

_____

b. About how many times per week does it occur?

c. About how long does each incident last?

d. Describe what happens *just before* the difficulty occurs.

_____

_____

_____

e. Describe what happens *just after* the difficulty occurs.

_____

_____

_____

Traditional Designs

APPROPRIATE APPLICATIONS

From an evidence-based practice perspective, the purpose of research is to understand which interventions and services are most effective with a client population in terms of attaining treatment goals. In order to confirm that research outcomes are truly the result of social work interventions, research designs must control for confounding factors, or other influences on client outcomes that may explain research findings. This chapter begins with a discussion of internal and external validity. *Internal validity* refers to how well the experiment controls for confounding factors—that is, factors other than worker interventions that could be responsible for therapeutic effects. *External validity* refers to how extensively the results can be generalized to other practice populations, contexts, and workers. The chapter then presents multiple designs and discusses their strengths and limitations with respect to internal and external validity.

CONTROL GROUPS

In order to control for confounding factors, research studies often examine outcomes of individuals who do not receive the intervention or service being evaluated. These individuals serve as a comparison or control group that, ideally, demonstrates how clients would do without the intervention. The outcomes for these clients can be compared with outcomes among those who receive the intervention (the experimental group) in order to draw conclusions about the impact of the intervention.

In constructing studies, one should, if at all possible, use random assignment of participants to experimental and control groups. This means that a given client is equally likely to be placed in the experimental or control group. A coin toss, for example, could be used to determine the client's assignment to one group or the other. Random assignment increases the likelihood that control group participants are as similar as possible to experimental group participants. Random assignment controls for the confounding factors described below that can influence a study, along with the variables of interest (Krause & Howard, 2003). An active control group is ideal, although a waiting-list control group may be more feasible. An active control group provides a baseline rate of improvement or deterioration over time, against which the experimental intervention can be compared and evaluated. To provide an accurate comparison, this control group should contain all the essential features of the treatment group except for the variables under investigation. For example, if we are evaluating task-centered casework, the control group should be similar in worker expectations for change, testing procedures, and context and length of sessions. An active control group provides a refined analysis of the components of effective treatment. However, such a fine analysis may be too costly in time, energy, and administration. A waiting-list control group consists of clients who have been placed on a waiting list for services in the agency. This group isolates the number of clients who improve through the passage of time without receiving documented professional help. Although the employment of an active control group is preferable, a waiting-list control group is often considered the minimal prerequisite for the adequate evaluation of treatment effects. Both groups should be offered services immediately after the collection of requisite data.

THREATS TO INTERNAL VALIDITY

Historical Effects

Historical effects are any factors or events that occurred at the same time treatment was initiated that could account for client outcomes. Some possible examples include the client receiving a raise, finishing an educational degree, or securing a divorce. When a control group is employed, however, such effects have the same probability of being present as in the experimental group. For this procedure to function adequately, the control group must be as similar as possible to the experimental group in all aspects (dimensions), such as race, age, sex, income, and so on, except for the operations involved in the provision of treatment. If the control group differs on relevant dimensions, the ability to rule out historical effects decreases.

Maturational Effects

If only one experimental group is used and is pre- and posttested without a control group, effects could be due to boredom, fatigue, participants getting older, or individuals getter better over time without treatment interventions. A control group isolates what is a normal rate of behavior change in outcome measures over time without therapeutic intervention. This rival hypothesis is particularly relevant for human service providers because accumulating research suggests that a substantial portion of clients with difficulties improve with the passage of time in the absence of therapeutic interventions (Bonanno & Lilienfeld, 2008; Chen, 2006; Cloud & Granfield, 2001). Similarly, a social work intervention may result in what appear to be only modest improvement in outcomes. However, a control group may illustrate that similar clients are likely to deteriorate over time and, thus, a modest improvement in outcomes is statistically and clinically significant in comparison with the control group. For example, a group of adolescents receiving a substance abuse prevention program may report no change in alcohol consumption during the course of the intervention. These findings imply that the intervention was not effective. However, a control group of students who receive no intervention may report significantly more alcohol use over time, indicating that the intervention may have influenced behavior, since the trend in the absence of intervention is to use more alcohol over time.

Testing Procedures (Pretest Sensitization)

Pretest sensitization is especially important in studies in which attitude change is a major outcome variable. Administering a test may sensitize clients to what you are interested in, especially if the studies deal with sensitive social topics, such as racism, marital satisfaction, and sexism. Testing alone can cause changes in people if individuals begin to think about appropriate responses. If control groups are used, this confounding factor may be identified and its effects isolated (Shadish, Cook, & Campbell, 2002).

Measurement Procedures

Problems can be caused by changes in calibration of measurement due to fatigue of data collectors, changes in testing procedures, and changes in manner of explaining instructions. One must control for the sex, age, and race of the person giving the questionnaire, and, in relevant instances, for time of year the questionnaire is administered. For example, students may respond differently to a measure of school satisfaction at the end of the school year than they would at the beginning or middle of the year. Moreover, one must ensure that interviewers ask questions consistently, dress appropriately, and present themselves similarly. If behavioral observers are used, they must be reliably observing the same behavior, and measurement procedures must be constant in pre- and posttests. Experimenter biases must be controlled for in the study. The researcher should not word questions in a way that could reveal the outcomes the interviewer seeks. Random assignment of different testers to experimental and control groups, videotaping administration of testing, audiotaping the instruction for the questionnaire if given in a group situation, and the execution of periodic reliability tests to assess how well the data collectors are executing their tasks all aid in controlling measurement difficulties (Rosenthal & Rosnow, 2007; Shapiro, 1971).

Statistical Regression Effects

How participants are selected for a study influences the outcome. If the most deviant group of a population is selected for study, some improvements will occur through time. Deviant individuals will reduce the frequency of unusual behaviors through time due to regression toward the average, otherwise known as statistical regression.

Differential Selection of Participants

If clients are not chosen for control groups in the same manner as for treatment groups, there is no way to isolate how the selection factors interact with treatment, and the effects may be attributed to the selection process. Use of random assignment is the best way to control for selection biases. However, this may not always be possible. In these situations, preexisting groups may be assigned to serve as intervention and control groups. For example, two seventh-grade classrooms may be participating in a study about bullying. Since the students cannot be randomly assigned to classrooms after the beginning of the school year, the researcher may choose one classroom to receive a bullying prevention program and another classroom to receive no intervention. There may be subtle, but important, differences between the students in these classrooms that could account for any differences in outcomes over the course of the study. Perhaps one teacher has a reputation for being highly effective in classroom management and addressing problem behavior; thus, the school may place children who have a history of behavior problems in her class. These preexisting differences between the groups mean that their behavior would look quite different over time in the absence of intervention. Thus, differences between these groups over time cannot be attributed to the intervention.

Experimental Mortality

Individuals who complete treatment may be substantially different from those who do not (Ahern & Le Brocque, 2005; Howing, Wodarski, Kurtz, & Gaudin, 1993). Attrition rates must be similar in experimental and control groups and should be kept under 30% in both groups to reduce confounding of data.

The seven factors described above affect the internal validity of a study (West & Thoemmes, 2010). They may operate singularly or in conjunction with one another. It is possible that a study might have multiple rival hypotheses operating to compromise its internal validity.

EXTERNAL VALIDITY

External validity relates to the relevance of research findings for populations that did not participate in the study. For example, an evaluation of a substance abuse treatment program in a large city that is implemented with predominantly low-income Latino men may not yield findings applicable to other populations, such as African American clients from rural communities. The many potential differences in cultural background and life experiences may result in different outcomes for these populations.

If the study lacks adequate internal validity, it is unclear whether the intervention is responsible for the observed outcomes, and the data cannot be generalized to other populations. Thus, internal validity is prerequisite to external validity. Some factors that may affect external validity include characteristics of the population, characteristics of the practitioners implementing the intervention, the organizational context, and multiple treatment interference.

Characteristics of the Population

If the participants included in a study are similar to the general population, the results are more likely to be generalizable. In contrast, external validity may be compromised if a study has specific, narrow selection criteria for the sample. For example, if a researcher decides that only clients with a particular diagnosis are eligible for participation in a study and excludes any clients with co-occurring disorders, the findings will not be generalizable to a typical community-based agency that serves clients with multiple presenting problems. The outcomes of clients with one identified mental health issue who receive the intervention may look very different from the outcomes of a client who is diagnosed with both a mental health disorder and a substance abuse disorder.

Characteristics of the Practitioners

If the practitioners implementing an intervention for a study have specialized training or credentials that make them different from most practitioners in community agencies, the study may have limited external validity. For example, a researcher may decide that facilitators should have a master's degree in social work, state licensure, and 5 years of post-master's clinical experience. An agency that employs mostly new social work graduates and has high rates of turnover may not be able to replicate the findings from the study in which the intervention was implemented by more experienced practitioners.

Organizational Context

Where the study is conducted has an effect on how the results can be generalized. Organizations differ on a number of relevant variables, including culture, climate, leadership, and resources. The study may need to include multiple organizations to increase the potential of the data for generalizing to other agencies.

Multiple-Treatment Interference

Although the effect of an intervention may be examined in isolation for a research study, community-based agencies typically offer a range of services to clients. The impact of an intervention may be influenced by the other services provided.

COMMON EXPERIMENTAL DESIGNS

Classical Design

In the following example, the basic objective of the classical design is to evaluate family therapy provided in a family service agency. That the independent variable (the therapist's intervention) and the dependent variable (the measure of change or outcome variables) are well specified is assumed. One hundred cases are available for the study: 50 are randomly assigned to treatment, and 50 are randomly assigned to a waiting-list control group. Both groups are pretested and posttested on the same outcome variables. Random assignment of clients equalized both groups on most of the variables that could confound a study, and the employment of pre- and posttest measures enables the assessment of the amount of change. The waiting-list control group provides the rate or level of change that can be expected in the clients over time. The major concern in such a design is that the testing mechanism itself may produce change in individuals. This concern may be more relevant for behavioral scientists, who do not work in human service agencies characterized by frequent employment of assessment batteries, to provide diagnostic information for choosing appropriate treatment interventions. In such agencies, testing effects would be minimal because clients are subjected to the procedure routinely. If a practitioner wishes to isolate the effects of the interaction of the assessment with the treatment, the Solomon four-group design, explained next, should be employed. Because this design doubles the number of experimental and control groups, the practitioner must consider the additional time, money, and administrative requisites involved.

Example of Classical Design

One hundred clients are randomly assigned:

1. Fifty clients assigned to experimental group: pretest, service, posttest.

2. Fifty clients assigned to waiting-list control group: pretest, no service, posttest.

Solomon Four-Group Design

The Solomon four-group design controls for pretest sensitization hypothesis, but it is costly because four groups are used instead of the traditional design of one experimental group and one control group. To isolate testing effects, one experimental group and one control group are pre- and posttested. The other experimental and control groups are posttested but not pretested. Random assignment of participants is essential because the assumption is made that all pretest scores would be similar if all groups were tested. To isolate the effects of testing, these pretest scores are used to calculate the differences between experimental and control groups that were pretested and those that were not pretested. Testing effects are isolated by noting the difference between the two control groups: one receives a pre- and posttest, and the other receives only the posttest. Through a similar process, this design also enables the isolation of testing and treatment interaction. The effects are isolated by comparing the differences between outcome variables in the two experimental groups, as illustrated below.

Example of Solomon Four-Group Design

Two hundred clients were randomly assigned to four different groups:

1. Fifty clients: pretest, no service, posttest

2. Fifty clients: no pretest, no service, posttest

3. Fifty clients: pretest, service, posttest

4. Fifty clients: no pretest, service, posttest

Multiple Groups Design

This design is utilized when the desire is to evaluate more than one treatment against others. In the future, studies will be executed that will evaluate the use of different interpersonal help approaches, such as problem solving, task-centered casework, or behavioral casework. As in the classical design, participants are pooled and are randomly assigned to experimental and control groups. The design allows for each treatment to be compared with the others but also permits the comparison of results against a control group. To elaborate on the classical design, a family service agency has 200 cases on which to execute the design; 50 each are randomly assigned to problem-solving casework, task-centered casework, behavioral casework, and a waiting-list control group. The rationale for the employment of the design is to determine which of two or more treatments is most effective and will produce the greatest change in the shortest period of time.

Example of Multiple Groups Design

Two hundred clients were randomly assigned to different casework approaches:

1. Fifty clients: pretest, problem-solving casework, posttest

2. Fifty clients: pretest, task-centered casework, posttest

3. Fifty clients: pretest, behavioral casework, posttest

4. Fifty clients: pretest, waiting-list for casework, posttest

Factorial Design

As knowledge about the phenomena social workers deal with increases in complexity, significant questions about effective treatment technologies and how to combine them with such things as worker attributes and contest variables to produce more efficient use of person power will be needed. Factorial designs in which variables are combined to isolate such interactional effects will ease the development of this complex knowledge.

In an evaluation of a community-based treatment program for children with antisocial behaviors, individual variables—treatment strategies, various types of group composition, and various degrees of worker training and combinations—were evaluated through a factorial sign to assess which variables had the greatest effect on children's behaviors.

Methods

A 3-x-3-x-2 factorial design was utilized. The first factor consisted of group-treatment strategies: social learning, traditional group work, and group centered. The second factor was group composition: antisocial, mixed, and prosocial. Each cell of the design was apportioned to enable evaluations of the third factor, degree of worker training—bachelor's-level (BSW) or master's-level (MSW) social workers. Such a design provides 10 combinations of the various variables that can be tested and whose effects can be isolated.

Participants

Thirty-six groups of children participated in the study. Of these groups, 12 consisted of children identified as antisocial, 12 consisted of one antisocial child and the remainder

TABLE 6.1 Examples of Factorial Design	Group Composition		
Treatment Program	**Antisocial**	**Mixed**	**Prosocial**
Behavior modification	2 MSW	2 MSW	2 MSW
	2 BSW	2 BSW	2 BSW
Traditional	2 MSW	2 MSW	2 MSW
	2 BSW	2 BSW	2 BSW
Group centered	2 MSW	2 MSW	2 MSW
	2 BSW	2 BSW	2 BSW

prosocial, and 12 consisted of prosocial children. Groups varied from 8 to 12 members, and participants were males ranging in age from 9 to 16 years. Antisocial children were defined as those who exhibit a high incidence of behaviors that disrupt interactional situations in which they participate. Prosocial children were defined as those who exhibit a low frequency of these behaviors (see Table 6.1).

Counterbalanced Design

In many instances, a research practitioner wants to evaluate a number of services but assignment of clients to a treatment or control group is not possible. In such instances, a counterbalanced design may be employed to provide an adequate evaluation. In this design, all clients are exposed to all the treatments for the same limited time period. In this design, clients are entered into all treatments in a random order. The process provides for the replication of the experimental effects, and experimental groups serve as their own controls.

In the following example, the counterbalanced strategy was utilized in gathering data to evaluate the effects of four reinforcement conditions receiving individual consequences, group-shared consequences, or varying combinations of the two on (a) peer tutoring, (b) arithmetic performance, (c) studying, (d) nonstudying, and (e) disruptive behavior. The study employed 60 experimental and 34 comparison children from three fifth-grade classes. To allow for clear specification of the effects of the four different reinforcement contingencies, a 4-x-4 counterbalance design was employed using four experimental groups and two comparison groups. This design protected against rival hypotheses that could account for the changes in the dependent variables. The four experimental groups were secured by dividing each of two experimental classrooms into two groups of randomly chosen children.

A 4-x-4 counterbalanced design was chosen because the children could not be placed in a pool and then randomly assigned to one of the four experimental groups. Students in each of the four experimental groups participated in four experimental conditions:

(a) students received only individual consequences, (b) students received 67% individual consequences and 33% group consequences, (c) students received 33% individual consequences and 67% group consequences, and (d) students received only group consequences. By entering all children into all treatments, the rival hypotheses of history, maturation, testing, instrumentation, regression, selection, and mortality that could be postulated to account for the data were controlled for. The design provided for the replication of the effects of the independent variables four times. The central idea is that if treatment effects are strong enough, they should occur each time the variable is introduced. This design also provided a way of dealing with the fact that the experimental groups started at different criterion levels on the dependent variables. The design was known to have confounding effects, but the replication feature provided a powerful test for the independent variables under the circumstances.

The above procedures were instigated when the original plan—utilization of all four of the fifth grades as experimental groups—had to be modified. This occurred because two of the teachers chose not to participate as experimental groups but volunteered only as controls. These were acknowledged not to be true control groups; because school had been in progress for 4 months, it was impossible to place all the students in a pool for random assignment into the traditional experimental and control groups. These comparison groups did not provide as much protection as would randomized control groups against the previously stated rival hypotheses that could be postulated to account for the changes in the dependent variables, but conducting the experiment in this manner was believed to be better because the comparison groups provided a criterion against which the progress of the experimental groups could be judged. It was understood that such a comparison would have limitations and that these limitations would have to be considered in evaluating the data provided by the experiment.

Each of the four experimental groups was in each of four treatment conditions (A–D) for 14 days and went through the four reinforcement contingencies in a randomized order, illustrated here in Table 6.2. The limitation of the counterbalanced design is the difficulty of isolating differential treatment effects from multiple interactions of treatments with the passage of time.

TABLE 6.2 Example of Counterbalanced Design				
Groups	**Order of Experimental Treatments**			
1	B	C	D	A
2	C	B	A	D
3	A	D	B	C
4	D	A	C	B
5 (comparison)	Baseline	Baseline	Baseline	Baseline
6 (comparison)	Pretest			Posttest

TREND ANALYSIS: A REPLICATION DESIGN

Trend analysis designs control for maturational effects through replication of the study. Current trends are compared with past or historical trends. In some cases, a researcher may compare trends in a population for several successive years. If similar significant results are secured each year, confounding factors can be ruled out. The following study is an example of a trend analysis design.

Underage drinking, or binge drinking (defined as having five or more drinks in a row), has become a major concern in our society. The increase in heavy drinking that occurs across the transition to college has increased professionals' awareness of a need for improved interventions to assist in the reduction of alcohol and substance use/abuse. At the University of Tennessee, a computer-based intervention was in place for the past 3 years, funded by the Substance Abuse and Mental Health Services Administration. The intervention was available to all college students via the university's computer network system and was completed mostly online. Students were given a computerized, standardized assessment of alcohol use, and then a brief intervention was provided based on the students' information. The intervention targeted students at highest risk for developing unsafe alcohol behaviors and/or increasing prior alcohol consumption habits in their first year of college. This intervention now has been provided to more than 54,000 graduate and undergraduate students, and since the launch of the program, binge drinking has dropped by 27% on campus. Further, frequent binge drinking dropped by 44%, and the number of liquor-law violations by 18- to 20-year olds decreased from 542 in 2004 to about 158 in 2007. Three yearly independent evaluations confirm similar trends in reduction of binge drinking and liquor-law violations. The project used trend analysis to demonstrate that the use of a computer technology to reduce and prevent college drinking has improved students' behaviors related to alcohol consumption.

Overview

As research practitioners consider the use of the traditional designs discussed here, the following critical question must be addressed: Has a practice technique or theory been isolated that warrants the time, personnel, and money involved in implementing a traditional design? This chapter has discussed several designs that are relevant for social work practice. Issues of internal and external validity were discussed as they relate to a researcher's ability to attribute outcomes to a targeted intervention and determine whether findings may generalize to other groups of clients.

Questions for Discussion

1.   Describe three strategies for reducing threats to internal validity in a study.

2.   A study conducted in a large urban school district examines the effectiveness of a bullying prevention program and employs a randomized design in which all

the middle schools in the district are randomly assigned to treatment conditions. Students in one school receive a school-wide bullying prevention program that includes students and school personnel. Students in a second school receive the same program, but a parent education component is also included. A third school receives no bullying prevention material. What are the strengths and limitations of the study with respect to internal validity AND external validity.

3. How could you use trend analysis to evaluate whether a new state tax on cigarettes is reducing cigarette use among adolescents?

References

Ahern, K., & Le Brocque, R. (2005). Methodological issues in the effects of attrition: Simple solutions for social scientists. *Field Methods, 17*(1), 53–69.

Bonanno, G. A., & Lilienfeld, S. O. (2008). Let's be realistic: When grief counseling is effective and when it's not. *Professional Psychology: Research and Practice, 39*(3), 377–378.

Chen, G. (2006). Natural recovery from drug and alcohol addiction among Israeli prisoners. *Journal of Offender Rehabilitation, 43*(3), 1–17.

Cloud, W., & Granfield, R. (2001). Natural recovery from substance dependency: Lessons for treatment providers. *Journal of Social Work Practice in the Addictions, 1*(1), 83–104.

Howing, P. T., Wodarski, J. S., Kurtz, P. D., & Gaudin, J. M. (1993). *Maltreatment and the school-aged child: Developmental outcomes and system issues.* New York: Haworth.

Krause, M. S., & Howard, K. I. (2003). What random assignment does and does not do. *Journal of Clinical Psychology, 59*(7), 751–766.

Rosenthal, R., & Rosnow, R. L. (2007). *Essentials of behavioral research: Methods and data analysis.* New York: McGraw Hill.

Shadish, W. R., Cook, T. D., & Campbell, D. T. (2002). *Experimental and quasi-experimental designs for generalized causal inference.* Boston: Houghton Mifflin.

Shapiro, A. K. (1971). Placebo effects in medicine, psychotherapy, and psychoanalysis. In A. E. Bergin & S. L. Garfield (Eds.), *Handbook of psychotherapy and behavior change.* New York: Wiley.

West, S. G., & Thoemmes, F. (2010). Campbell's and Rubin's perspectives on causal inference. *Psychological Methods, 15*(1), 18–37.

CHAPTER 7

Designs for Daily Practice Evaluation

The previous chapter reviewed traditional designs and discussed how these designs control for confounding factors. This chapter focuses on time-series designs and how they can be used to inform practice decisions. In terms of administrative execution, time, personnel, and money, time-series designs are easy to implement. Their role in research is to provide beginning knowledge about practice techniques and theory; they produce preliminary data as to whether interventions should be evaluated more formally. Such knowledge supplies the empirical rationale for practice.

The use of a research design in empirical practice is justified by the need to know: Did my interventions make a difference for this client? In technical terms, this means obtaining data to indicate whether interventions were effective, while controlling for as many confounding factors as possible that might influence therapeutic outcome. The major aim is to keep all conditions constant except those in which the practitioner is interested.

It frequently has been assumed that the only way therapeutic services can be evaluated is through the employment of classical experimental designs—those in which participants are assigned randomly to one or more experimental or control groups. However, such designs may not be the most appropriate for the initial evaluation of services. They may be costly in money, energy, and administrative time (Bloom, Fischer, & Orme, 2009). Initial use of classical designs in practice research violates one of the basic tenets of research: execute the requisite pilot studies before undertaking large evaluations. Moreover, the criterion of random assignment of participants in traditional designs is usually hard to meet in the evaluation of services provided. Single-case studies and time-series designs overcome many of these difficulties. These approaches can be easily implemented in social work; they are economical in terms of money and energy required to implement them, and they are uncomplicated in administrative execution. Above all, single-case studies and time-series designs provide data that will enable workers to determine if their interventions have had an effect on client behaviors and provide the foundation data for the decision to engage in sophisticated designs involving control groups, the major aim of which is to present conclusive data on the effectiveness of services.

In the traditional experimental design, clients are grouped into experimental and control groups, although this process is diametrically opposed to a basic practice assumption that every individual is unique and should be considered in his or her own gestalt. The single-case study, on the other hand, may alleviate many of the measurement problems discussed. In this approach, clients serve as their own control, and their change is evaluated against data they provide during a baseline period preceding the application of treatment. The single-case study methodology also alleviates the moral and legal aspects of placing clients in a no-treatment control group. It is too early to predict the effects of various legal decisions on the use of a traditional no-treatment control group in practice evaluation research; however, the use of this methodology may be challenged in the future on two legal bases: denial of the right to treatment and denial of equal protection to the client (Bloom et al., 2009).

The time-series designs described in the classic clinical research literature provide practitioners with tools they can utilize in their everyday practices to evaluate the effect of their practice interventions on clients (Bloom et al., 2009). These designs—which include the ABAB, AB, and multiple-baseline designs—can be implemented easily in social work. The time-series designs are economical in money, energy, administrative execution, and personnel required for implementation. Thus, their accessibility to practitioners for the evaluation of their practice interventions is significant.

THE ABAB DESIGN

The classical single-case study of the time-series format is the ABAB design, which consists of four basic phases in which behaviors are observed for a specific time period. In the first phase, the client is exposed to a baseline period. During this period, the worker does not rationally plan interventions likely to influence the display of target behaviors. After the client's observed incidence of target behavior reaches a stabilized or "natural" level, the behavior-change strategy is introduced. In the second phase, the client's behavior is monitored until it is once again stabilized. A behavior is considered stabilized when the average of its measurements does not vary more than 10% for 3 to 5 days. After the behaviors stabilize, a baseline condition is reintroduced in the third phase. This condition is termed the *reversal period*. The procedure enables the practitioner evaluating the changes to determine whether the influence attempt was responsible for the various changes in behavior; it clearly reduces the number of confounding factors that could account for the behavior changes. Immediately after it becomes evident that the strategy has been effective in reducing the target behavior, the treatment procedures are applied once again in the fourth phase. In many instances, a follow-up phase has been added to the ABAB design, thus providing the opportunity to determine how lasting the changes were.

The data presented in Table 7.1 provide an example of the ABAB design used to evaluate group-work service provided to one fifth-grade, antisocial child in one facet of the St. Louis study (Wodarski, Feldman, & Pedi, 1976).

Percentage frequencies of prosocial, nonsocial, and antisocial behavior were graphed for the entire group of children, who met at a community center for 2-hour sessions over a period of 14 weeks. An ABAB design was implemented because it met the structured program requirements of the agency and provided for the systematic evaluation of treatment efficacy.

TABLE 7.1	Average Percentage of Nonsocial, Prosocial, and Antisocial Behavior for One Child, According to Four Experimental Conditions			
	Experimental Condition			
Type of Behavior	**Baseline**	**Reinforcement**	**Reversal**	**Reinforcement**
Prosocial	66.00	92.00	80.00	93.00
Nonsocial	16.50	4.75	1.50	7.00
Antisocial	17.50	3.25	18.50	0.00
	100.00	100.00	100.00	100.00

The group workers were trained in several behavior modification techniques. Specifically, they were taught to utilize positive reinforcement and group contingencies to increase the incidence of prosocial behavior and to use mild punishments and extinction to decrease the incidence of antisocial behavior (Feldman, Caplinger, & Wodarski, 1983). Initial training consisted of a 3-hour seminar during which behavior modification techniques were presented and discussed. In the latter part of the seminar, role-playing was used to demonstrate the application of these techniques. The group worker held weekly conferences with a supervisor to discuss implementation of the techniques. In addition, consultations were held periodically with various behavior modification specialists. Reinforcers, such as candy, money, free play time, and special field trips, were used along with other inducements more readily available at the community center, such as access to the gym or pool. Sequentially, the experimental group underwent the first baseline condition for 4 weeks, the first reinforcement condition for 6 weeks, the reversal condition for 2 weeks, and the experimental reinforcement condition for 2 weeks. For more rigorous experimental evaluation, it might have been useful to expand the duration of the last reversal and experimental reinforcement conditions; however, it was necessary to modify the program to fit within the agency's prestructured calendar. Such modifications are basically inimical to an individualized treatment program and should be avoided if possible.

A unique nonparticipant observation technique was devised to measure the frequency of prosocial, nonsocial, and antisocial behavior exhibited by the children. This procedure seldom has been implemented in relatively open settings, such as community centers. A trained observer was placed in the group 3 weeks before the baseline period so members could adapt to the observer's presence before data was gathered. The observer was instructed to remain as unobtrusive as possible to avoid virtually all social interactions with the members. On introduction, the children were informed that observers would not interfere in any way with the group, that all information to be obtained by them would be kept confidential and would be reviewed only by the research team, and that they could help the observers do their job by ignoring them.

A checklist titled "Behavioral Observational Scale for Children and Therapist Interacting in a Group," which yielded highly reliable data, was used to tabulate the respective incidence of prosocial, nonsocial, and antisocial behaviors observed (Wodarski & Feldman,

1976). Checklist reliability was established through simultaneous ratings of behavior recorded on videotapes illustrating the small-group behavior of similar children. The tapes included numerous illustrations of antisocial behavior. Observers also were trained with videotapes. The training sessions were completed when each observer could reliably agree on behavioral coding with one of the investigators and with other observers at a level of 0.90 or above, utilizing the rating categories later described. An agreement criterion of 0.90 or above was required. Observations were made in a fixed order every 10 seconds for 1 of the 10 children, then for another child, and so on, until all the children had been observed. The procedure was repeated for the duration of each group meeting. In each 10-second time frame, the first behavioral act observed for a child was rated as prosocial, nonsocial, or antisocial. To ensure consistent agreement among observers, individual reliability checks were performed for their ratings at six separate points during the program.

BEHAVIORAL CATEGORIES

Definitions

Antisocial Behavior

Antisocial behavior was defined as any behavior exhibited by a group member that disrupts, hurts, or annoys other members, or that otherwise prevents members from participating in the group's tasks or activities. These might include gross motor behaviors, physical contacts, verbalizations, object interference, or other such behaviors. No effort was made to differentiate qualitatively the extent to which each particular behavior could be classified as antisocial. Instead, the importance of the recording scheme adheres in its capacity to tabulate systematically obvious antisocial behaviors according to a time-sampling format and, consequently, to calculate relatively accurate frequencies of antisocial, prosocial, and nonsocial behaviors per unit time for each child. Moreover, in conjunction with the data presented below, the format permits an approximation of the proportion of total behaviors observed for each child that are antisocial, prosocial, and nonsocial in nature.

Prosocial Behavior

Prosocial behavior was defined as any behavior exhibited by a group member that helps the group complete a task or behavior, or that otherwise exemplifies constructive participation in the group's activities. Illustrative prosocial behaviors include instances in which a given child helps another, demonstrates skills, provides others with materials or objects necessary for participation, asks the group leader to help someone who is experiencing difficulty, requests others to engage in the group's activities, positively reinforces others' task participation, and similar actions.

Nonsocial Behavior

All behavior cannot be categorized solely as prosocial or antisocial. In many instances, children temporarily withdraw from group activity without either helping or disrupting others. In the present study, nonsocial behavior was defined as any behavior exhibited by a group member that is not directly related to the group's ongoing activity. Such behavior is neither directed toward helping the group complete a task nor toward disrupting, hurting, or annoying others participating in the group's activities. Relevant illustrations include staring out a window or into space, laying one's head on a piece of furniture, and playing or remaining alone while others are engaged in a group activity.

Results

Prosocial Behavior

The data presented in Figure 7.1 indicate that the average incidence of prosocial behavior exhibited by the group members increased at the first introduction of reinforcement

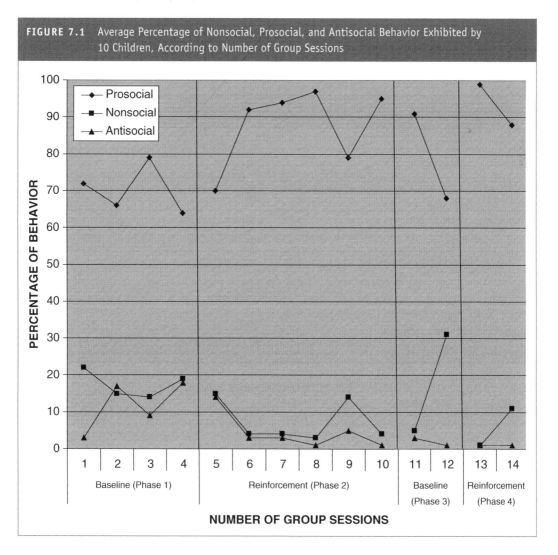

FIGURE 7.1   Average Percentage of Nonsocial, Prosocial, and Antisocial Behavior Exhibited by 10 Children, According to Number of Group Sessions

contingencies. During the reversal period, the incidence of prosocial behavior dropped to about 69% at the end of that period. In contrast, prosocial behavior rose to its highest point when the contingencies were reintroduced. The differences between the baseline and reinforcement conditions are significant (F = 20.88; df = 1,56; p < 0.05). The statistical evaluation procedures are expounded in Chapter 8.

Nonsocial Behavior

With the first introduction of reinforcement contingencies, nonsocial behavior was reduced, and during the next reversal period, it continued to fall. When contingencies were reintroduced, the incidence rose. It is evident that nonsocial behavior was reduced considerably after the first baseline period but was not appreciably reduced thereafter. Although the incidence of nonsocial behavior increased, this increase was not statistically significant; therefore, it may well represent a fluctuation within normal limits. Unfortunately, relatively little empirical data exist regarding normative rates of nonsocial behavior for children's groups. Such data would be useful for child-care workers and, accordingly, represents a useful subject for future field research.

Antisocial Behavior

Antisocial behavior was reduced during the first baseline period. At reversal, it rose, and no antisocial behavior was recorded during the last two periods. The differences between the baseline and reinforcement conditions are statistically significant (F = 11.20; df = 1,56; p < 0.05). The data regarding antisocial behavior reflect only the frequency of acts observed; qualitative features of the behavior were not measured. Many of the antisocial behaviors that occurred at low frequencies, such as jumping out a window and hitting others, were highly disruptive for children, whereas other behaviors were of lesser consequence. These data, along with less systematic data obtained from post-experimental conferences with the group worker and clinicians who informally observed the group, suggest that the treatment just described brought about a significant reduction in virtually all types of antisocial behavior demonstrated by the children. This is all the more striking because the program was conducted within the context of an open and fluid community setting. Post-program discussions with the group leader and other personnel within the agency suggested that the program also yielded a number of other positive results, including stronger friendship relations, greater peer cooperation, and more effective accomplishments of group objectives. Data from multicriteria measures have indicated a positive evaluation of the intervention.

Interventive Methods

Space limitations precluded the full presentation of requisite graphs, statistical tests, and discussions for each child. Instead, the average incidence of prosocial, nonsocial, and antisocial behaviors exhibited by all 10 group members are depicted in Figure 7.1. For illustrative purposes only, data are presented in Table 7.1 for a child whose behavioral profile was considered representative of the group members. Before examination of these data, a brief summary of the child's behavioral characteristics and subsequent treatment contingencies is provided.

A Case Illustration

Stan is a 10-year-old boy in the fifth grade of a school system considered one of the most progressive in the St. Louis metropolitan area. His parents are relatively affluent. Stan appears to be of normal height, weight, intelligence, and health for his age. Stan's behaviors during the baseline and reversal periods included pushing peers and throwing furniture at them, running in the halls, disrupting other groups by name-calling and making loud noises, and nonparticipation in group activities. Diagnosis revealed that the foregoing antisocial behaviors were reinforced by positive reinforcement from peer attention, particularly from his pal Bill. This included supportive laughter, joining Stan in such behavior, and physically reinforcing him with pats on the back and smiling. Additionally, it was apparent that the group worker's reprimands to Stan tended to reinforce such behavior rather than diminish it, particularly by reaffirming Stan's position of preeminence within the peer group.

Contingencies of behavioral change were implemented after baseline. The worker began by engaging the group in an activity that the members found particularly enjoyable. This practice is common to virtually all effective group therapies and, regardless of any theoretical basis, tends to enhance the worker's attractiveness and capabilities as a therapeutic agent. However, as in previous instances, Stan and Bill attempted to disrupt the activity. Because the majority of members wished to engage in the activity, the group worker reinforced them for constructive participation with smiles and praise (positive reinforcers) and ignored the behaviors of Stan and Bill (extinction). Shortly thereafter, the disruptions of Stan and Bill ceased and they began to participate constructively in group activities. However, extinction represents a viable change strategy only as long as the target members' disruptive behaviors do not entail significant stress or harm for their peers. In this case, as nonthreatening disruptive behaviors diminished, the group worker reinforced the members' prosocial behavior through smiles, verbal praise, and other reinforcing acts. In instances in which disruptive behaviors entail greater stress, other techniques of behavioral change such as time-out, punishment, stimulus control, and positive reinforcement of prosocial behaviors should be implemented to facilitate the attainment of group tasks (Wodarski, 2009; Wodarski & Feit, 1994).

To enhance the members' efforts to build cooperative relationships and plan and complete increasingly difficult tasks, the group worker paired the children with one another in subsequent sessions and structured further group contingencies. Specifically, the members were told that each person would earn 20 cents if the group could plan an activity in which everyone could participate. They were also informed that each member would receive an additional 20 cents if everyone participated in the chosen activity. In almost all instances of contingency construction and instruction, the members agreed with this regimen. Such contingencies helped Stan plan and participate more effectively and consistently in group activities. The group contingency increased peer pressure on Stan and others to participate in the chosen activity; each group member's reinforcement was contingent on his or her own participation and that of others. Additionally, as they earned social reinforcements from the worker and from their peers, the members were more comfortable in the group. To avert satiation of monetary reinforcements, other group contingencies and reinforcers were introduced at periodic intervals. For example, the group was asked to engage in a given activity without any one member disrupting the others, after which the members could have a special party, go swimming, or enjoy refreshments. As members' prosocial behavior increased, all forms of reinforcement and behavioral contingencies, including group contingencies, were gradually phased out, thus making the treatment environment more comparable with other peer groups in the open community.

Data provided in Table 7.1 on Stan's prosocial, nonsocial, and antisocial behaviors correspond with data in Figure 7.1. Data show an increase in prosocial behavior and a decrease in antisocial behavior during reinforcement periods. Nonsocial behavior showed a steady decline until the last reinforcement period. The group data presented in Figure 7.1 and individual data presented in Table 7.1 show nicely how practice interventions can be evaluated through the use of the ABAB design. The conclusion of the agency program schedule limited the ability to secure follow-up data. Such data would have permitted a strong evaluation of intervention effects. Another design that can be used in instances when it is not possible to engage another baseline condition is the AB design. Actually, it is the first half of the ABAB design. The AB design involves securing a baseline and introducing treatment after the behavior to be altered is stabilized. This is a minimum prerequisite to demonstrate the intervention's effect on treatment goals. However, such an evaluation is not as strong as the evaluation offered by the ABAB design because the AB design does not control for as many biasing factors.

THE MULTIPLE-BASELINE DESIGN

In many practice situations, the ABAB design may not be feasible due to the types of behaviors being modified or for various ethical reasons. The primary reason for utilizing an alternate design is that in the ABAB design, the modified behavior usually will not reverse itself because it is maintained now by natural reinforcements existing in the client's environment. Also, in certain instances, reversals would be too damaging to the client or significant others in his or her life. For example, when fighting is brought under control in a home, when marital partners decrease the frequency of their interpersonal altercations, or when abusive parents develop better child-discipline skills, it will not be feasible to do a reversal on this behavior since physical harm has been inflicted on others in the past.

A design that may be utilized in lieu of the ABAB design is the multiple-baseline design, wherein a series of behaviors for modification are operationalized. Predictions are made on how the various techniques will affect different behaviors. Each behavior is then modified according to a time schedule. Usually, one or two behaviors are modified at a time. For example, the worker might want to decrease such behaviors as yelling, fighting, throwing objects, and straying from the group, and increase prosocial behaviors such as task participation and appropriate verbal comments. The worker in this instance might choose first to ignore the yelling and use positive reinforcement to increase appropriate verbal comments. Once the yelling had decreased and the appropriate verbal comments had increased, the worker would sequentially modify the second, third, and fourth behaviors.

In Table 7.2, an outline is provided of how such a process operates. The technique employed becomes more efficacious every time the behavior changes in the directions predicted for the child; that is, the scientific concept of replication rules out other factors that neglect the responsibilities for the change. Table 7.2 illustrates the application of a multiple-baseline design by practitioners who evaluated the use of task-centered casework to improve mother–child communications.

TABLE 7.2 Example of Multiple-Baseline Design		
Behavior		**Time Period at Which Modification Plan is Instituted[c]**
Antisocial[a]	**Prosocial[b]**	
Not sitting with group	Task participation	1
Yelling	Appropriate speech	2
Fighting	Helping behavior	3
Throwing objects	Cleaning up	4

[a]Extinction used to decrease

[b]Positive reinforcement used to increase

[c]Length of time periods, not specified, depends on how rigorous one wants to be in showing the effects of the modification plan. A period usually lasts until the behavior stabilizes at a variance of less than 10% point variability for 3 to 5 days.

Purpose of the Intervention

The client is a divorced 26-year-old woman primarily supported by public welfare. She has three children, ages 5, 3, and 1. The client stated that she was having difficulty understanding the speech of her 3-year-old son, who was being treated for lead poisoning at a pediatric hospital—a 62-bed, long-term care facility for children up to 18 years old. The speech department at the hospital tested his skills and found them to be slightly above average for his age level. Therefore, the authors, in consultation with the speech department and the mother, decided to teach the mother various language skills, with the aim of increasing the son's verbal skills and the mother's understanding of her son's verbalizations.

Rationale for Intervention

Task-centered casework was chosen because it is a structured intervention that details the role of the therapist and client in specific terms. The client stated that she had problems understanding the child and was not familiar with the stages of a child's verbal development. The researchers felt that a structured interaction between the mother and child based on specific verbal-skills training would increase the mother's understanding of the child's speech and help the child acquire requisite verbal skills. Unfortunately, many lower-income individuals do not have adequate models, resources, or knowledge of how to teach their children verbal skills. With task-centered casework, both the mother and the child learned within a structured task situation.

The client's difficulties fit one of the seven target typologies Reid and Epstein (1972) discuss: difficulty in role performance. Reid and Epstein state that clients with perceived problems in role performance are aware of a gap between how they execute their roles and how they would like to execute their roles. The mother could not understand how her son's verbal abilities were above average when she could not always understand him.

The verbal learning tasks were designed to enhance her execution of her parent role. Briefly, the three demonstration tasks for the mother were naming an object, describing the function of an object, and verbalizing commands clearly.

An important justification for using task-centered casework is the research support demonstrating positive outcomes in improving behavior (Colvin, Lee, Magnano, & Smith, 2008; Kinnevy, Healey, Pollio, & North, 1999). Tolson (1977) used a multiple-baseline design to systematically evaluate the intervention across three targeted behaviors seen as creating communication problems for a couple. Tolson's study was also the only study that targeted improved communication using task-centered casework. However, communication between parent and child was not investigated in any study. In such cases, when there is no established evidence supporting the use of an intervention for a targeted behavior with a particular client, evaluating the intervention's effectiveness is essential.

Method

It was hypothesized that task-centered casework would increase a mother's communication skills with her child. The independent variable is task-centered casework. Conceptually defined, task-centered treatment is a short-term model of social work practice deigned to alleviate specific problems of individuals and families (Reid, Abramson, & Fortune, 1992). The operational definition can be stated in a step-by-step progression: The client's problems are explored, a target problem is identified, a task is formulated, time limits are structured to attain casework goals, work on the task is carried out, and termination is effected. As stated in *Webster's New World Dictionary* (Agnes & Agnes, 2003), *communication* means "to give or exchange information," and *skills* means "expertness that comes from training, practice, and so forth." Skills the child learns are the dependent variables, such as identifying objects, explaining the function of an object, and responding to verbalized commands.

When determining the target problem, the authors used the format in *Task-Centered Casework* (Reid & Epstein, 1972). The problem with which the client was concerned was explored first. More than any other problem, the mother discussed her communication difficulties with her 3-year-old child. This problem was defined in behavioral terms. In this case, the mother said that when he was excited and wanted to tell her something, she could not understand his verbalizations. The authors, therefore, classified the target problem in the typology of difficulty in role performance as difficulties in communicating with a child.

The Verbal Language Development Scale, by Mecham (1971), was given to the mother to assess what she thought her child's verbal-skills level was. The scale revealed that the mother did not think her child's verbal behaviors were appropriate for his age level. Her assessment was shared with the speech department to help determine the appropriate skills to teach the child. The speech department, the researchers, and the mother agreed that the tasks focused on should increase the child's ability to identify objects and to explain their functions and should increase his responsiveness to verbal commands.

For the first baseline session, the authors met with the mother in the play kitchen of the hospital's preschool nursery. The mother was instructed to make a dinner with her son for 10 minutes in the play kitchen, a setting familiar to the child. The authors observed and tape recorded the baseline frequency of the three verbal task skills. After this session, the mother was told that the first skill she would perform was object identification.

For the first interventions with the child, the mother was to make a dinner in the same play kitchen with her son's help. She was instructed to point out objects in the kitchen and state, "This is a pot [pitcher/fork/refrigerator]." The authors first modeled the expected behaviors and then the mother rehearsed them, with the authors repeating the original instructions. The mother then made a play dinner with her son for 10 minutes.

For the second intervention, the mother was instructed to describe the function of an object while making dinner with her son: for example, "The refrigerator keeps food cold," "The broom sweeps dirt," and "The pot cooks food." The authors modeled the task; the mother rehearsed it and carried it out.

For the third intervention, the verbal skills she would be using with her son were again explained. The mother was informed that the third task would be to verbalize two commands, such as "Get the broom from the closet and sweep up the dirt," or "Get the dolls from their bed and put them in high chairs." Expressing two commands at the same time gives the child an opportunity to use and develop a more complex cognitive skill: remembering one command while carrying out the other. The authors modeled the skill, the mother rehearsed it to an acceptable level, and the intervention was carried out. After each session, the authors measured the frequency of each task by using a tape recorder. The authors required 100% agreement among themselves for reliability on criterion behavior.

At the conclusion of the three intervention sessions, the results of the study were summarized for the mother. She was encouraged to discuss any problems she had during the intervention or problems she might have when using the skills in the future at home. Two follow-up sessions were executed—one 5 days and the other 3 months after the conclusion of the study—to measure the maintenance on all three levels. The overall design of the experiment is outlined in Table 7.3.

Results

Baseline

Baseline frequencies of the respective behaviors were 9 occurrences of object identification, 3 of description of function, and 6 of the performance of two commands (see Figure 7.2).

TABLE 7.3   Multiple-Baseline Design According to Phases

Communication Problem	Day					
	1	**4**	**8**	**14**	**19**	**109**
Name	Baseline	Intervention			Follow-up I	Follow-up II
Function	Baseline	Baseline	Intervention		Follow-up I	Follow-up II
Command	Baseline	Baseline	Baseline	Intervention	Follow-up I	Follow-up II

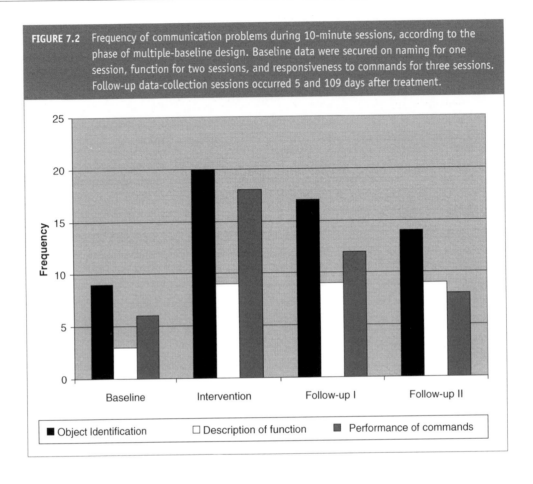

FIGURE 7.2 Frequency of communication problems during 10-minute sessions, according to the phase of multiple-baseline design. Baseline data were secured on naming for one session, function for two sessions, and responsiveness to commands for three sessions. Follow-up data-collection sessions occurred 5 and 109 days after treatment.

Intervention

Task performance was greatest during each respective intervention. The data on task performance in Figure 7.2 show that for task 1, there was an increase in the occurrence of the targeted behavior from a frequency of 9 to 20; for task 2, from a frequency of 3 to 9; and for task 3, from a frequency of 6 to 19. For all tasks, performance improved significantly from baseline to intervention.

Follow-up

Data in Figure 7.2 show that for verbalizing the function of an object, the child's follow-up scores were stable compared with the treatment phase. Both follow-up values equaled 9. A decrease occurred for naming an object in the first and second follow-ups and for responsiveness to commands. However, scores were still higher than baseline rates. The follow-up data on naming an object and on responsiveness to commands suggest that additional casework sessions might have been warranted; but the client felt this was unnecessary.

Overview

All the foregoing designs–the ABAB, AB, and multiple-baselines designs—are feasible for practitioners in community settings. The actual design of any study depends on the context of the behavioral-change situation in terms of behaviors to be altered, time and treatment considerations, and administrative concerns.

These pilot projects illustrate how practitioners can use research to evaluate practice and, thus, increase their confidence in their effectiveness; that is, one may observe the demonstrated significant impact on client behaviors. Empirical knowledge is essential for any profession. The ABAB, AB, and multiple-baseline time-series designs provide a clinical research methodology that can be easily implemented by practitioners and used to improve practice. Thus, the divisions between researchers and practitioners may be narrowed through the use of the discussed methodologies (Bloom et al., 2009).

It is apparent that the designs discussed will be applied to evaluate various practice interventions on a larger scale within the foreseeable future. The outcome of such a process inevitably will be that the knowledge base of social work practice becomes increasingly complex, and only then will it be able to reflect and cope effectively with the immensity of those problems social workers typically face. Moreover, knowledge can be developed by replication of study by different researchers; replication controls for many different biasing factors.

Questions for Discussion

1. Describe the presenting problem of a client in behavioral terms.

2. Identify a measureable goal for your work with this client.

3. Identify three strategies for measuring progress toward reaching this goal.

4. How often would you use these measures?

5. What are the advantages and disadvantages of the frequency of measurement identified above?

6. How would you proceed if your measures indicated a lack of progress?

References

Agnes, M., & Agnes, M. (Eds.). (2003). *Webster's new world dictionary* (4th ed.). New York: Pocket.

Bloom, M., Fischer, J., & Orme, J. G. (2009). *Evaluating practice: Guidelines for the accountable professional* (6th ed.). Boston: Allyn & Bacon.

Colvin, J., Lee, M., Magnano, J., & Smith, V. (2008). The Partners in Prevention Program: The evaluation and evolution of the task-centered case management model. *Research on Social Work Practice, 18*(6), 607–615.

Feldman, R. A., Caplinger, T. E., & Wodarski, J. S. (1983). *The St. Louis conundrum: The effective treatment of antisocial youth.* Englewood Cliffs, NJ: Prentice Hall.

Kinnevy, S. C., Healey, B. P., Pollio, D. E., & North, C. S. (1999). Bicycle works: Task-centered group work with high-risk youth. *Social Work With Groups, 22*(1), 33–47.

Mecham, M. J. (1971). *Verbal language development scale.* Circle Pines, MN: American Guidance Service.

Reid, W. J., Abramson, J. S., & Fortune, A. E. (1992). *Task strategies: An empirical approach to clinical social work.* New York: Columbia University Press.

Reid, W. J., & Epstein, L. (1972). *Task-centered casework.* New York: Columbia University Press.

Tolson, E. R. (1977). Alleviating marital communication problems. In W. J. Reid & L. Epstein (Eds.), *Task-centered practice* (pp. 147–156). New York: Columbia University Press.

Wodarski, J. S. (2009). *Behavioral medicine: A practitioner's guide.* New York: Haworth.

Wodarski, J. S., & Feit, M. D. (1994). Applications of reward structures in social group work. *Social Work With Groups, 17,* 123–142.

Wodarski, J. S., & Feldman, R. A. (1976). Behavioral observational scale for children and therapist interacting in a group. In O. G. Johnson (Ed.), *Tests and measurements in child development: Handbook II* (pp. 1168–1171). San Francisco: Jossey-Bass.

Wodarski, J. S., Feldman, R. A., & Pedi, S. J. (1976). Reduction of antisocial behavior in an open community setting through the use of behavior modification in groups. *Child Care Quarterly, 5,* 198–210.

CHAPTER 8

Application of Statistical Techniques in the Evaluation of Practice

This chapter examines the use of statistical procedures that enable us to evaluate the effectiveness of practice. The aim is not to provide a background in statistics; the reader is assumed to have a working knowledge of statistical methods. The intent here is to provide examples of the application of appropriate procedures in the evaluation of research for practice. The more sophisticated multivariate techniques are discussed in Chapter 9.

Statistical procedures are tools that help decide whether research results are meaningful or significant enough to apply in social work practice or theory. Two assumptions are made in regard to statistical procedures: (a) there is order to the universe, and through systematically studying the phenomena of interest, knowledge will be developed; and (b) only a limited number of events are related to one another. Simply stated, statistics help us describe and put into order the phenomena dealt within social work. The major aim of statistics is to find consistency in the data of interest.

DATA DESCRIPTION

Measures of central tendency permit us to make meaningful statements about data that have been depicted in the manner mentioned above. The central tendency is a characteristic of a distribution of scores or values that tells us where these scores or values tend to cluster. Three common measures of central tendency—the mean, median, and mode—quickly communicate the focal points of the data. The mean is the average score, or the sum of all scores divided by the total number of scores; the median is the point at which 50% of the scores or values fall below and 50% above; and the mode is the most frequently occurring score or value. These descriptive procedures are frequently used in pilot research. For example, in a study that described the competencies mental health workers need in

123

order to work with the elderly in rural areas, data were secured through interviews with 15 practitioners who worked in a variety of agencies. Once the data were secured, descriptive statistics were used to present the data as knowledge needed for practice. The information centered on agency operational procedures, psychological and sociological aspects of aging, physiological aspects of aging, treatment modalities, and administrative tasks.

Table 8.1 shows how the mean can be used to quickly communicate what competencies social workers felt were the most and least necessary for workers who provide services to the elderly in rural areas. Descriptive statistics also were employed in the studies reviewed in Chapter 7. There, descriptive statistics were used to summarize the considerable amount of data collected on the behavior of the participants in the group in relationship to the various experimental conditions, as well as to depict the behavior of one child.

TABLE 8.1 Responses of Practitioners Regarding Necessary Competencies for Providing Mental Health Services to the Aged in Rural Areas

Respondent	Agency operational procedures	Psychological aspects of aging	Psychological and sociological aspects of aging	Treatment modalities	Administrative
1	3	5	1	2	4
2	4	2	1	3	5
3	3	4	1	2	5
4	4	2	1	3	5
5	4	2	3	1	5
6	1	3	2	4	5
7	4	2	1	3	5
8	2	3	1	4	5
9	3	4	1	5	2
10	4	1	2	3	5
11	4	1	2	3	5
12	4	3	1	2	5
13	3	5	1	2	4
14	4	1	3	2	5
15	4	2	1	3	5
Mean	3.8	2.6	1.4	2.8	4.6

Note: Scores rated on a scale of 1 (most important) to 5 (least important).

Another valuable descriptive statistic that facilitates workers' practice endeavors is standard deviation (SD). SD is used to describe the amount of variation in the data—that is, how the data group themselves around the average score. For instance, assume that in the intake process, workers at a community mental health center used a 25-item scale to measure depression. SD allows the practitioners to compare individual scores. It provides data on the percentage of individuals who score within one, two, and three SDs. Each of the 25 items has five possible responses; therefore, an individual can score anywhere from 0 to 125. A mean of 75 and an SD of 10 would indicate that 68.26% of scores are between 65 and 85. Likewise, 95.44% of the scores would fall within two SDs, or between 55 and 95. Finally, 99.74% of all scores would fall between 45 and 105, or three SDs. In this case, SD can help determine whether the individual needs treatment.

BASIC STATISTICAL FUNCTIONS

In addition to describing data, statistical operations can perform three other basic functions: (a) indicate how closely variables are associated with one another, (b) tell us whether significant differences exist between groups, and (c) indicate the amount of variation in one variable that is related to variation in another. Statistical operations range from simple analyses—such as bivariate analyses measuring the association between two variables or testing the differences between groups—to complex operations involving determination of the association among many variables or development of a prediction equation from representative data.

Beginning knowledge generally is developed through the use of correlational statistics and statistics that determine whether significant changes have taken place in the phenomena of interest. Refinement of knowledge occurs with the use of statistics that delineate exact relationships between variables. Thus, the employment of progressively stringent statistical procedures could be considered a sequential process in the knowledge-building process.

STATISTICAL CORRELATIONS

In many areas of empirical practice, only beginning knowledge is available on which variables are associated with the phenomena of interest. Statistics that indicate association are correlational; they reveal how strongly variables are related to one another. Various assumptions have to be made concerning measures of the variables, and appropriate correlational techniques are then chosen depending on whether the data are nominal, ordinal, interval, or ratio level.

Correlational studies examine relationships among variables but cannot be used to determine whether change in one variable causes change in another. For example, students may report whether or not they have received substance abuse prevention programming in school. They may be asked on the same survey to report about their attitudes regarding substance use and their substance use behaviors. A correlational study may examine whether students who report having participated in a prevention program also report less substance use. Even if students who participated in a prevention program report less use, this analysis cannot be used to determine whether participation in a prevention program causes a reduction in substance use. It may be that those students were less likely to use substances before they participated in the prevention program.

In social work research, correlational studies have been used to explore how environmental factors are associated with individual outcomes, in keeping with the person-in-environment perspective. Rosenthal, Wilson, and Futch (2009) used a correlational analysis to determine the relationship of exposure to traumatic events, protective factors, and psychological distress among 1,066 adolescents. Traumatic events included witnessing or experiencing a violent incident or the loss of a significant friend or relative. Protective factors included social supports and perceived self-efficacy. Their findings indicate that traumatic events and protective factors were associated with psychological distress but that protective factors were more strongly associated with distress than traumatic events were. Thus, experiencing traumatic events was associated with increased distress, while the presence of protective factors was associated with decreased distress. The presence of protective factors was more strongly associated with distress than the traumatic events were. The implications of this study are that both protective factors and traumatic events are related to psychological distress; however, because the study is correlational, the researchers cannot conclude that the traumatic events or protective factors predict or cause psychological distress.

In another example, correlational data has helped determine characteristics of men who abuse their female partners, including depression, alcohol abuse, financial stress (Peek-Asa et al., 2005), low self-esteem, feelings of inadequacy, hostility, feelings of powerlessness, and traditional views of sex roles (Dwyer, Smokowski, Bricout, & Wodarski, 1995). Although correlational data cannot be used to conclude that these characteristics cause abuse, they may be useful in identifying couples who are at risk for domestic violence and developing programs geared toward prevention (Dwyer et al., 1995; Peek-Asa et al., 2005).

t-TESTS

A t-test determines whether two groups are significantly different on some variable of interest. The test uses the mean scores on the variable in determining whether the groups are different. An independent-samples t-test compares mean scores of two different groups at one point in time. For example, Hopson and Lee (2011) used a t-test to compare students from low-income and higher-income families on academic performance and social supports. T-test analyses compared academic achievement and social supports for students who were eligible for free and reduced-price lunches and for those who were not eligible. The results indicate that students who were eligible for free and reduced-price lunches reported poorer grades and behavior and fewer social supports at home and in their neighborhoods than students who were not eligible (Hopson & Lee, 2011).

A paired-samples t-test is used when comparing individuals in one group at two points in time. For example, a group of clients may receive an intervention to improve social skills, and an evaluator or practitioner may want to know whether the clients' social skills have improved after participating in the group intervention. Thus, the clients could complete a pretest measure of social skills prior to receiving the intervention and a posttest following completion of the intervention. A paired-samples t-test allows for pairing the pretest and posttest scores for each individual in the group to determine whether social skills have improved.

Cook et al. (2006) used a paired-samples t-test analysis to determine whether participation in a 1-day training resulted in changes in service delivery among 424 medical and mental health service providers immediately following the training and 1 year later. The training focused on mental health implications of living with HIV and AIDS. The results indicate that participants in the training reported a significant increase in the delivery of HIV services to HIV-positive clients 1 year following the training (Cook et al., 2006).

ANALYSIS OF VARIANCE

When more than two groups of clients are studied, the appropriate evaluation procedure is the analysis of variance (ANOVA). The ANOVA, which is similar to the t-test, enables the investigator to simultaneously compare more than two groups. Whereas the t-test analyzes whether means for clients in two groups are significantly different, an ANOVA analyzes whether there are significant differences among multiple groups in terms of the variation in mean scores. More specifically, the ANOVA determines whether the difference among clients across different groups is greater than the difference among clients within the same group.

In one example, Kim and Moon (2007) examined the needs of 123 family members caring for stroke patients in rehabilitation settings in South Korea. The needs were measured by the Family Needs Questionnaire. The questionnaire measures caregivers' needs related to health information, emotional support, instrumental support, professional support, and support in the community. Caregivers indicate the importance of each perceived need and the degree to which each need has been met. The researchers compared satisfaction among caregivers of patients in outpatient clinics, inpatient facilities, and day hospitals. The ANOVA in this case examines whether satisfaction scores differed significantly for caregivers whose patients were receiving care in different facilities. The results indicate that caregivers caring for patients in outpatient clinics were the least satisfied in terms of receiving health information, emotional support, and professional support, compared with those caring for patients in inpatient facilities or day hospitals (Kim & Moon, 2007).

A repeated-measures ANOVA can be used to examine group differences over time. Claiborne (2006) employed a repeated-measures ANOVA to investigate whether a care-coordination intervention results in improved outcomes for stroke survivors. Thirty-three patients in an inpatient physical rehabilitation program who had suffered a stroke were randomly assigned to receive either the care-coordination intervention or the normal treatment provided by the inpatient program. Patients completed the Short Form–36, which measures quality of life in physical and mental health domains, at baseline and at 3 months. The findings indicate that the patients who received the care-coordination intervention experienced significantly greater improvements in quality of life on the mental health domain than patients who received the normal care without this intervention. There were no differences between groups in the physical health domain (Claiborne, 2006).

ANALYSIS OF COVARIANCE

In many instances, research executed to evaluate human services employs groups that are significantly different in outcome variables at the outset. Groups often cannot be restructured for purposes of the study because of agency operating procedures. In such situations, clients cannot be assigned randomly to experimental and control groups to control for initial differences. Changes in the experimental group cannot, therefore, be evaluated against a comparison group without employing a statistical procedure that can correct for initial differences. The analysis of covariance (ANCOVA) procedure provides the opportunity to control for such initial differences. An ANCOVA is basically an ANOVA that controls for pretest scores by including them in the analysis as covariates. For example, if antisocial behavior is an outcome criterion, children can be measured during a baseline period and during treatment and follow-up. The baseline measure of antisocial behavior can be used as a covariate.

In one study (Wodarski & Pedi, 1978), ANOVA and ANCOVA were used to evaluate two group-treatment strategies against a control-treatment strategy based on the behaviors exhibited by antisocial children, those of their therapists, and two self-rating scales. For the first year, 139 antisocial children were stratified according to age and then randomly placed into 14 groups. For the second year, 100 children were placed into 11 groups composed of antisocial children. Behavioral measurements of the children's and therapists' behaviors were secured at each weekly 2-hour meeting.

For the data depicted in Table 8.2, ANCOVA was used to adjust for initial differences in baseline scores and to control for significant variables that could be postulated to account for the results, such as age, worker style, superior style, dropouts, and methodological factors of observer and tester style. This statistical technique provided for the evaluation of the experimental treatments through analysis-of-change scores between time 1 and time 2, with adjustments made for initial group differences at time 1. Thus, this technique provided the opportunity to assess what changes took place in clients after treatment was introduced. The testing procedure initially consisted of evaluating general factors, such as treatment methods. When the F scores were significantly different, additional analyses specifically assessed which levels of the factors were significantly different; that is, the procedure evaluated each treatment against the others to determine exactly where the differences lay.

REGRESSION ANALYSIS

An important goal of research is the isolation of those variables related to the phenomena being studied. If this is possible, then the subsequent ability to influence the phenomena is increased. Regression analysis enables researchers to determine how certain variables are related to one another in their prediction of a phenomenon; it permits isolation of those variables that are significantly related to the phenomena of interest and enables the specification

TABLE 8.2   Behavioral Data in Terms of Average Incidence of Prosocial, Nonsocial, and Antisocial Behavior for Baseline (B) and Treatment (A), According to Treatment Method and Year

Treatment Method	Number		Behavior Category											
			Prosocial				Nonsocial				Antisocial			
	1st Year	2nd Year	1st Year		2nd Year		1st Year		2nd Year		1st Year		2nd Year	
			A	B	B	A	B	A	B	A	B	A	A	B
Behavior Modification	59	32	0.91	0.91	0.90	0.94	0.05	0.04	0.02	0.01	0.04	0.05	0.07	0.05
Traditional	42	21	0.90	0.90	0.96	0.97	0.06	0.03	0.04	0.02	0.04	0.07	0.00	0.01
Controlled Treatment	36	37	0.90	0.94	0.97	0.95	0.05	0.03	0.02	0.02	0.05	0.04	0.05	0.03

Note: The baseline consisted of an average of 6 meetings, and the treatment period consisted of an average of 22 meetings. The controlled treatment groups served as a baseline for the entire study. Additional regular ANOVA tests in which the data were analyzed according to three time periods after treatment, consisting of the mean of six consecutive meetings each, yielded no significant differences for treatment. Similarly, the use of participants who had a 5% higher incidence of antisocial behavior during baseline for both the ANCOVA and regular ANOVA yielded no significant difference.

of the magnitude of the various relationships. A simple regression analysis may include one independent variable (or predictor variable) and one dependent variable. Multivariate regression analyses include multiple predictor variables and are discussed in Chapter 9.

Regression analysis is similar to a correlation analysis but allows the researcher to predict future values of a variable based on the values of another variable. For example, a practitioner may be interested in predicting students' future school performance based on parental involvement in school, such as attending school events and parent-teacher conferences. You could use a regression analysis to predict the future grades of students based on their parents' current level of involvement.

Regression analysis can help social workers isolate variables relevant to child abuse, family violence, and marital discord. Such knowledge will be crucial in developing the preventive approach in social work. For example, regression analysis can isolate those children who are at risk during the divorce process by age, gender of the child, length of marital discord, time of divorce in relation to the developmental cycle, number of siblings, race, children's perception of the divorce process, and family income. Ultimately, the procedures will facilitate the planning of appropriate interventions.

Overview

It is most important for social workers to remember that statistics are tools to be used to enhance practice. The concept of statistical significance determines whether the associations, differences, or relationships between variables are meaningful or strictly caused by chance. Statistics enable empirical social workers to determine whether variables isolated through research are relevant in helping clients. As practitioners begin to incorporate these skills in their repertoires, the future will witness a more sophisticated application of statistical procedures and, thus, the development of a more elaborate knowledge base. On the basis of this knowledge, the social worker will derive the complex interventions necessary to help clients.

Questions for Discussion

1. Review the findings of a study presented in a research article. Review the research methods, analysis, findings, and conclusions. Write a statement that summarizes the findings in terms that would make it useful for your client.

2. How would you apply critical thinking in examining the analysis presented in a research article?

3. Imagine that you read a correlational study examining the relationship between student–teacher relationships and student behavior. The author states that "the findings of the study indicate that students who have more positive relationships with teachers have fewer behavior problems in the classroom. Thus, increased teacher support is likely to result in improved behavior."

   a. What additional information would be helpful in evaluating the accuracy of these statements?
   b. How would you decide whether to use this information in making practice decisions with children in schools?

References

Claiborne, N. (2006). Effectiveness of a care-coordination model for stroke survivors: A randomized study. *Health in Social Work, 31*(2), 87–96.

Cook, J. A., Razzano, L. A., Linsk, N., Dancy, B. L., Grey, D. D., Butler, S. B., et al. (2006). Changes in service delivery following HIV/AIDS education of medical and mental health service providers: Results of a one-year follow-up. *Psychiatric Rehabilitation Journal, 29*(4), 282–288.

Dwyer, D. C., Smokowski, P. R., Bricout, J., & Wodarski, J. S. (1995). Domestic violence research: Theoretical and practice implications for social work. *Clinical Social Work, 2,* 185–198.

Hopson, L. M., & Lee, E. (2011). *Mitigating the effect of poverty on academic and behavioral outcomes: The role of school climate in middle and high school.* Manuscript submitted for publication.

Kim, J. W., & Moon, S. S. (2007). Needs of family caregivers caring for stroke patients: Based on the rehabilitation treatment phase and the treatment setting. *Social Work in Health Care, 45*(1), 81–97.

Peek-Asa, C., Zwerling, C., Young, I., Stromquist, A. M., Burmeister, I. F., & Merchant, J. A. (2005). A population-based study of reporting patterns and characteristics of men who abuse their female partners. *Injury Prevention, 11*(3), 180–185.

Rosenthal, B. S., Wilson, W. C., & Futch, V. A. (2009). Trauma, protection, and distress in late adolescence: A multideterminant approach. *Adolescence, 44*(176), 693–703.

Wodarski, J. S., & Pedi, S. J. (1978). The empirical evaluation of the effects of different group-treatment strategies against a controlled-treatment strategy on behavior exhibited by antisocial children, behavior of the therapist, and two self-ratings measuring antisocial behavior. *Journal of Clinical Psychology, 34,* 471–481.

CHAPTER 9

Advanced Statistical Techniques in Social Work Research

This chapter provides an overview of advanced statistical methods that can be applied effectively in social work. These evaluative tools can be used to isolate or find correlations among variables that may be influencing treatment. The data obtained can be used to create or improve intervention strategies. For example, if a clinician were to develop a program to discourage smoking among adolescents, a pre-intervention questionnaire could be administered to gather and analyze information on factors that describe these individuals—such as income, peer group, socioeconomic status, and school performance—using advanced statistical methods. This information could serve a dual purpose: first, to assist in the assessment of the population and, second, to help in the design of an effective intervention. Several evaluative methods can determine the nature, strength, and direction of the relationship between variables. These tools help researchers develop questions for further study and help clinicians in their practice. The procedures to be discussed include multivariate analysis of variance, discriminant analysis, path analysis, structural equations, factor analysis, canonical correlations, multivariate regression analysis, and meta-analysis.

MULTIVARIATE ANALYSIS OF VARIANCE

Multivariate analysis of variance (MANOVA) extends the analysis of variance (ANOVA), discussed in Chapter 8, to several dependent variables. Unlike ANOVA, MANOVA determines whether statistically significant differences exist between two or more groups based on the group members' scores on the set of dependent variables rather than on one single variable. The MANOVA, therefore, is a more powerful evaluative tool.

In social work practice, this type of procedure can be useful. For example, an agency wishes to study the attitudinal biases of the staff. Three groups could be divided based on length of time working: less than 1 year, more than 1 year, and longer than 2 years. Several dependent variables could be tested using written questionnaires to describe attitudes toward different types of clients. Dependent variables to be measured might include perceived gender differences in attitude toward minority clients, perceptions of age, and religious affiliation. Using a MANOVA, data could be collected and analyzed to observe any potential professional biases, promote agency awareness, and facilitate any necessary changes in policy or staff.

Corcoran (2006) used MANOVA to compare engagement and behavioral outcomes for 237 children receiving solution-focused therapy and traditional treatment, or treatment as usual, at a mental health clinic sponsored by a school of social work. Parents and children completed self-report measures of their behavior at pretest and posttest. Children also indicated their level of engagement in treatment. MANOVA was used to determine whether students receiving solution-focused therapy differed from students receiving traditional treatment in their behavior over time. In other words, the analysis examined whether the behavior of students in one group changed more dramatically than the behavior of students in the other group between pretest and posttest. The MANOVA analysis allowed for including multiple dependent variables related to engagement and behavior in the same analysis. Findings from the study indicated that children receiving either solution-focused therapy or traditional treatment improved in their behavior. No significant differences between groups appeared over time in behavioral reports from parents or in children's self-reports of behaviors. While both groups improved, the group receiving solution-focused therapy did not improve more than the other group (Corcoran, 2006).

DISCRIMINANT ANALYSIS

Discriminant analysis is a technique used to analyze multiple interval- or ratio-level independent variables and identify which of those variables or variable combinations best predict a nominal-level dependent variable. It allows for investigating differences between two or more groups based on a group of variables. The independent variables are used to classify individual cases into one of the groups in the analysis. In one example, Eastman (2005) used discriminant analysis to examine variables associated with treatment completion among adolescent sex offenders. Participating adolescents belonged to one of three categories: offenders who were entering treatment, those who had completed treatment, and those who began treatment but failed to complete it. Participants completed measures of cognitive distortions associated with sexual assault of children, sexual knowledge, attitudes about sexual behavior, empathy, and self-esteem. Using discriminant analysis, Eastman (2005) identified variables that were able to distinguish adolescents who completed treatment from those who did not. The presence of cognitive distortions that justified sexual offenses had the strongest ability to distinguish between these groups. Other important variables included level of intellectual functioning, history of witnessing domestic violence, and history of personal victimization (Eastman, 2005).

PATH ANALYSIS

While ANOVA and MANOVA are statistical tools designed to describe correlations in dependent variables, path analysis demonstrates the complexity of relationships through the use of models. A visual model is used to depict variables, with arrows indicating which variables have direct and indirect effect on others. When a variable has an indirect effect on dependent variables, it is called an intermediary variable, because it is affected by one variable and has an effect on the dependent variable. The diagram depicting the string of variables and their effect on other variables is called a "path." Path analysis allows for an intervention to be diagrammed so the potential impact of various factors within treatment can be predicted (Rubin, 2007).

Path analysis is a relevant tool for therapists who wish to generate practice-oriented theories to describe certain characteristics of human behavior. Path analysis can compare a model of presumed direct and indirect relationships among several variables with observed data in a study. In other words, the research can determine whether the model represents a good fit for the data. If the fit is close, the model is retained and used or further tested. If the fit is not close, the model will be revised or a new model will be tested (Loether & McTavish, 1974). Using path analysis, practitioners are better able to relate theory and practice because this technique allows for strength and direction of variables to be observed in treatment.

An example of path analysis can be found in Figure 9.1, which is a diagram of an analysis that examined the impact of several intervention strategies designed to reduce antisocial behavior. This type of graph is useful for two reasons: first, the actual interventions are documented, and second, the predicted or actual impact on youth behavior is recorded. This data can be analyzed to observe which factors were most effective in treating the client population and, if applicable, generalized to other intervention settings.

Neely-Barnes, Marcenko, and Weber (2008) used path analysis to examine the relationships between predictor and intermediate variables and community inclusion among individuals with mild and severe intellectual disabilities. The predictor variables were choice, or the extent to which individuals were able to make their own choices in their daily routines, and living arrangement, or the number of other individuals with an intellectual disability in their household. Community inclusion was measured through involvement in community activities, such as shopping, dining, and entertainment. This study is an

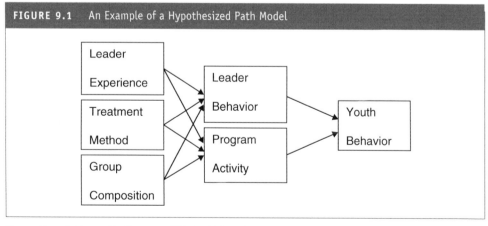

FIGURE 9.1   An Example of a Hypothesized Path Model

Source: From Feldman, Caplinger, and Wodarski (1983), p. 219.

example of multiple-group path analysis because it examined whether group membership (mild vs. severe disability) moderates the relationship among the variables. The findings indicated that individuals with mild disabilities experienced more choice and were more likely to live independently than those with severe disabilities. In addition, choice and the number of other individuals in the household were strong predictors of community inclusion for those with a mild disability but not for those with a severe disability (Neely-Barnes et al., 2008).

STRUCTURAL EQUATIONS

Whereas path analysis analyzes relationships between measured variables, structural equation modeling (SEM) allows for examination of latent variables along with measured variables. Measured variables can be observed or measured directly. Latent variables are not measured directly but are estimated in the model from measured variables, which are assumed to capture the latent variable constructs. When two or more measured variables covary, they may imply the presence of a latent variable. Often in social work, practitioners find themselves attempting to measure behaviors or cognitions that do not easily lend themselves to being objectively monitored. SEM permits the researcher to study latent variables by incorporating measures of related concepts that are more easily observed to represent changes or improvements in the variable of interest, which is not directly observable. In one study, for example, items on a scale that asked clients about whether they had protection against being robbed, had access to law enforcement, and lived in a safe community were used to measure the latent variable, perceived safety (Perron, Alexander-Eitzman, Gillespie, & Pollio, 2008).

Similarly, structural equations could be helpful in trying to measure the degree of motivation of high school students applying to enter baccalaureate programs. School performance, school attendance, preparation for entrance exams, individual career interests, and ability to use problem-solving skills could be used as indicators of varying levels of motivation. However, since any quantitative tool may possess some degree of error, several measured variables are needed to represent the latent variable, motivation.

SEM can accommodate multiple interrelated dependence relationships in the same model; it can estimate multiple interrelated equations simultaneously. Thus, the dependent variable in one equation can be the independent variable in another (Hair, Anderson, Tatham, & Black, 1998). SEM has many practical applications for practitioners because they frequently measure the progress of clients on outcomes that are not directly observable, such as degrees of anger, levels of frustration, or anxiety. SEM allows for measuring these constructs and including them in an analysis, even when they were not directly measured through a preexisting scale, for example.

SEM was used in a cross-sectional study examining the influence of victimization on depressive symptoms in more than 9,600 homeless and mentally ill adults (Perron et al., 2008). The model included relationships between victimization and two latent variables: depressive symptoms and perceived safety. The researchers employed confirmatory factors analysis (see next section) to examine the fit of the latent variables by studying the factor loadings of the measured variables into the constructs of depressive symptoms and perceived safety. They found that the models exhibited good fit. In examining the path relationships, the researchers found that nonphysical victimization was associated with higher levels of depressive symptoms but was not associated with perceived safety. Conversely, physical victimization was associated with lower levels of perceived safety but was not associated with depressive symptoms. In addition, perceived safety partially mediated the relationship between victimization and depressive symptoms. Thus, homeless individuals who have been victimized may have more depressive symptoms because they feel less safe (Perron et al., 2008).

FACTOR ANALYSIS

Another powerful analytical technique, known as factor analysis, is able to analyze the extent to which a group of variables are correlated with one another. Specifically, this method is used to determine the number and nature of underlying constructs, called factors, among a larger set of variables. Factor analysis can locate the common factors within a group of variables and, therefore, minimizes the data to be analyzed. For example, if multiple variables are related to self-esteem, they are likely to correlate highly with one another. These variables could be combined into a single variable, self-esteem, rather than measuring each variable separately. By regrouping the information, a more organized and focused data evaluation can be accomplished. Best of all, this type of procedure allows for the observance of patterns in data, which can be used in future research or intervention strategies. The technique is often used to group together items on measurement scales and to assess their validity.

Cunningham, Duffee, Huang, Steinke, and Naccarato (2009) used factor analysis to assess the reliability and validity of a newly developed scale designed to measure engagement among youth in residential treatment centers. The researchers examined multiple variables—readiness to change, bonding with staff, and collaboration with staff—and predicted that these items would be related to one another and could serve as a measure of engagement in treatment. The results of the study indicate that all items on the questionnaire loaded on the same factor, suggesting that they measure the same construct, which the research team labeled "engagement" (Cunningham et al., 2009).

CANONICAL CORRELATION

Another analytical tool, canonical correlation, is used to investigate the relationship between two sets of variables when each set consists of at least two variables. It allows for examining the impact of a set of variables on another set of variables. This procedure can investigate the following questions (Thompson, 1984):

1. To what extent can one set of two or more variables be explained by another set of two or more variables?

2. What contributions does a single variable add to the explanatory power of the set of variables to which the variable belongs?

3. To what extent does a single variable contribute to predicting or explaining the composite of the variables in the variable set to which the variable does not belong?

4. What different dynamics are involved in the ability of one variable set to explain different portions of the other variable set?

The mathematical side to this method is extremely complicated; however, canonical correlations are useful because they provide information on the relationships between different data sets and the individual variables within sets of data. Unfortunately, any practical use of this procedure requires a large number of participants to ensure validity. The analysis is meant to reveal relationships across different measures and determine which groups of variables independently predict other variables, with minimal redundancy.

One study used canonical correlation to examine the relationship between groups of risk factors and the patterns of service intervention for 239 cases involved with child protective services (Jagannathan & Camasso, 1996). The Washington Risk Assessment Matrix was the measure of risk, and case records were used to obtain data on services provided. The analysis revealed three distinctive risk profiles that received different types of services: older children with behavior problems, children from disadvantaged households, and children with an unemployed parent. According to the findings, services to older children with behavior problems were characterized by unsuccessful phone calls but few unsuccessful home visits. Home visits to children from economically disadvantaged households tended to be unsuccessful, and supervisors were less involved. Services to children of unemployed parents tended to be longer, more intense, and involve supervisors. Thus, certain combinations of risk factors predicted different levels of services from caseworkers (Jagannathan & Camasso, 1996).

MULTIVARIATE REGRESSION ANALYSIS

As discussed in Chapter 8, regression analysis enables researchers to determine how certain variables are related to one another in their prediction of a phenomenon; it permits isolation of those variables that are significantly related to the phenomena of interest, and enables the specification of the magnitude of the relationships among variables. When the regression equation includes multiple predictor variables, a multivariate regression analysis, or multiple regression, is employed to analyze the data. The aim is often to identify which variables are the best predictors of the dependent variable (Rubin, 2007).

Simmel (2007) used multiple regression to examine the relationship between risk and protective factors and behavior problems among 273 adopted foster children. The risk and protective factors in the analysis included age of placement, number of placements, history of physical and sexual abuse, history of neglect, prenatal exposure to substances, and parental readiness for adoption. Parents completed the Behavior Problems Index repeatedly during three waves of data collection. The first wave of data was collected 2 years following adoption, the second was collected 4 years following adoption, and the third was collected 8 years following adoption. Findings indicate that behavioral scores during the first wave of data collection strongly predicted behavioral scores during successive waves.

During the first wave of data collection, history of neglect was a strong predictor of negative behavior. History of sexual abuse and multiple foster placements remained significant predictors of behavior problems during wave two, and placement in multiple homes was the only pre-adoption risk factor that remained significant during the third wave. Parental readiness was also a significant mediating variable influencing the behavioral outcomes of the youth (Simmel, 2007).

In another study examining the behavior of 251 antisocial children at a community center, six predictors were employed: self-inventories filled out by referral agents, parents, children, leaders, and observers, and a subclass of the Jesness Inventory (1969) filled out by the children and designed to measure self-reported tendency toward manifest aggression. The Manifest Aggression Scale consists of 31 items. Jesness contends that these items reflect an awareness of unpleasant feelings, especially anger and frustration; a tendency to react readily with these emotions; and other obvious discomfort concerning the presence and control of these feelings. Data presented in Table 9.1 indicate that for both years of the study, the checklist filled out by the behavioral observer explained the greatest amount of variance in the incidence of antisocial behavior exhibited by the children at the community center during baseline. The amounts of variance explained for the first and second years were, respectively, 0.3213 and 0.2513. The checklist filled out by the leader of the children's group yielded the next greatest amount of explained variance, 0.0522 and 0.0992 for the first and second years, respectively. For the first year, the child's checklist yielded a significant amount of explained variance: 0.0180. This finding did not hold true for the second year (Wodarski & Pedi, 1978).

META-ANALYSIS

Meta-analysis is a technique grounded in the assumption that effect sizes in different studies are comparable. Effect sizes are measures of the strength of the relationship between variables, and they are expressed in standardized terms that allow for comparing effect sizes across multiple studies. This permits the synthesis of findings from multiple studies

TABLE 9.1 Amount of Variance Explained by the Various Predictors in Baseline Antisocial Behavior at the Community Center, According to Each Year of the Study

Independent Variables	Percentage of Variance		Change in Proportion of Variance	
	1st Year	**2nd Year**	**1st Year**	**2nd Year**
Observer checklist	0.3213	0.2513	0.3213	0.2513
Leader checklist	0.3735	0.3505	0.0522	0.0992
Child checklist	0.3915	n.s.	0.0180	n.s.

Note: n.s. = not significant. Only variables that predict a significant amount of the variance are included in the table.

and, ultimately, practice recommendations (Nugent & Ely, 2008). The approach calculates the mean effect size across multiple studies that examine the same variables. It can also be used to calculate the aggregated statistical significance of findings from multiple studies. Because it synthesizes the results from multiple studies, meta-analysis is a tool that can simplify the practitioner's responsibility to examine research findings on a particular presenting issue or client population. In addition, the meta-analysis provides the practitioner with a sense of the size of an intervention's effect. For example, Durdle, Gorey, and Stewart (2008) used meta-analysis to assess the strength of the relationship between obsessive-compulsive disorders and pathological gambling across 18 different studies. The results indicated a strong relationship, with an effect size of 1.01, between pathological gambling and obsessive-compulsive traits.

The utility of meta-analysis findings is based on the assumption that effect size estimates are directly comparable (Nugent & Ely, 2008). However, variability in the reliability and validity of measures and other methodological issues often make it difficult to argue that effect sizes are truly comparable. Therefore, findings from meta-analytic studies are often subject to scrutiny if they do not provide a great deal of detail about the procedures for each study included in the analysis (Nugent & Ely, 2008).

Another potential problem occurs when some studies are not included in a meta-analysis because they were not published, for example. Because studies with null findings may be less likely to be published, neglecting to include unpublished studies could result in the appearance that an intervention is more effective across multiple studies than it actually is. One intervention that raises such questions is multisystemic therapy, which has demonstrated effectiveness in numerous well-controlled clinical trials published in scholarly journals. Yet, when unpublished studies were included in a systematic review of the research on multisystemic therapy, Littell, Popa, and Forsythe (2005) found that it was no more effective than alternative treatments. A meta-analysis of multisystemic therapy studies would be misleading if these unpublished studies were not included.

Despite these potential limitations, meta-analysis can be a useful tool for evaluating the effectiveness of aggregated studies on a particular intervention and is often recognized as the best evidence on intervention effectiveness (Lam & Kennedy, 2005; Nugent & Ely, 2008). It can also promote the use of evidence-based practice by providing an efficient means of educating oneself about the existing research on an intervention.

Overview

This chapter has reviewed many multivariate analysis procedures often used in research relevant for social work practice. Although social workers may not be in a position to use the analyses described in this chapter, it is still imperative that they develop a basic understanding of these tools so they may become informed consumers of the research. As more practitioners are able to review literature and test the findings in practice, their work will challenge researchers to develop more effective theories for assessment and intervention in social work practice.

Questions for Discussion

1. A mental health agency surveys its clinical staff about morale, job satisfaction, frequency of supervision, and perceptions about the quality of supervision. The agency is interested in whether clinicians who have frequent supervision and are more satisfied with the quality of their supervision report better morale and job satisfaction than other clinicians.

   a. What type of statistical analysis would be appropriate?
   b. What are the strengths and limitations of this analytical approach?

2. Review the statistical analysis section of a research article and discuss the following:

   a. Does the analytical approach seem appropriate for the research questions?
   b. What are the strengths and limitations of the analytical approach?
   c. What other types of analysis would also be appropriate for the research question, if any?
   d. How would the quality of information obtained from different analytical approaches differ?
   e. Do the conclusions drawn in the article seem appropriate given the analytical approach? Why or why not?

References

Corcoran, J. (2006). A comparison-group study of solution-focused therapy versus treatment-as-usual for behavior problems in children. *Journal of Social Service Research, 33*(1), 69–81.

Cunningham, W. S., Duffee, D. E., Huang, Y., Steinke, C. M., & Naccarato, T. (2009). On the meaning and measurement of engagement in youth residential treatment centers. *Research on Social Work Practice, 19*(1), 63–76.

Durdle, H., Gorey, K. M., & Stewart, S. H. (2008). A meta-analysis examining the relations among pathological gambling, obsessive-compulsive disorder, and obsessive-compulsive traits. *Psychological Reports, 103*(2), 485–498.

Eastman, B. J. (2005). Variables associated with treatment failure among adolescent sex offenders. *Journal of Offender Rehabilitation, 42*(3), 23–40.

Feldman, A. R., Caplinger, E. T., & Wodarski, J. S. (1983). *The St. Louis conundrum: The effective treatment of antisocial youths.* Englewood Cliffs, NJ: Prentice Hall.

Hair, J. F., Anderson, R. E., Tatham, R. L., & Black, W. C. (1998). *Multivariate data analysis* (5th ed.). Upper Saddle River, NJ: Prentice Hall.

Jagannathan, R., & Camasso, M. J. (1996). Risk assessment in child protective services: A canonical analysis of the case management function. *Child Abuse and Neglect, 20*(7), 599–612.

Jesness, C. F. (1969). *The Jesness Inventory manual.* Palo Alto, CA: Consulting Psychologist Press.

Lam, R. W., & Kennedy, S. H. (2005). Using meta-analysis to evaluate evidence: Practical tips and traps. *Canadian Journal of Psychiatry, 50,* 167–174.

Littell, J., Popa, J. H., & Forsythe, B. (2005). Multisystemic therapy for social, emotional, and behavioral problems in youth aged 10–17. *Campbell Collaboration Review, 2.* Retrieved November 10, 2006, from http://www.campbellcollaboration.org/doc-pdf/Mst_Littell_Review.pdf

Loether, H. J., & McTavish, D. G. (1974). *Descriptive statistics for sociologists: An introduction.* Boston: Allyn & Bacon.

Neely-Barnes, S. L., Marcenko, M. O., & Weber, L. (2008). Community-based, consumer-directed services: Differential experiences of people with mild and severe intellectual disabilities. *Social Work Research, 32*(1), 55–64.

Nugent, W. R., & Ely, G. E. (2008). Variability in meta-analytic effect sizes and meta-analysis outcomes as a function of measurement procedure: A simulation study. *Best Practice in Mental Health, 4*(2), 80–98.

Perron, B. E., Alexander-Eitzman, B., Gillespie, D. F., & Pollio, D. (2008). Modeling the mental health effects of victimization among homeless persons. *Social Science and Medicine, 67*(9), 1475–1479.

Rubin, A. (2007). *Statistics for evidence-based practice and evaluation.* Belmont, CA: Thomson.

Simmel, C. (2007). Risk and protective factors contributing to the longitudinal psychosocial well-being of adopted foster children. *Journal of Emotional and Behavioral Disorders, 15*(4), 237–249.

Thompson, B. (1984). *Canonical correlation analysis: Uses and interpretations.* Beverly Hills, CA: Sage.

Wodarski, J. S., & Pedi, S. J. (1978). The empirical evaluation of the effects of different group treatment strategies against a controlled treatment strategy on behavior exhibited by antisocial children, behaviors of the therapist, and two self-rating scales that measure antisocial behavior. *Journal of Clinical Psychology, 34*(2), 471–481.

CHAPTER 10

Development and Use of Information Management Systems for Human Services

A Practical Guide

Social and political events have demonstrated the necessity of establishing human services based on data that provide the rationale for the planning and delivery of services, evaluation of data, and fiscal support. Moreover, status indicators for the human services have changed. In the 1950s and 1960s, an agency had status if it employed a psychoanalyst as a consultant. Today, status is determined by an agency's capacity to use data on services and client outcomes as evidence to inform quality improvement efforts. Information management systems are an important tool that builds capacity for using research evidence in decision making.

Agencies are finding that lack of resources no longer prevents the introduction of new technology. However, as in all fields, the application of technology often lags behind its development. This chapter addresses the development and implementation of information management systems pertinent to helping agencies provide appropriate services to clients. Also reviewed is the role of information systems in human service agencies—as related to managerial applications, client descriptive analyses, diagnosis, treatment planning, documentation of program implementation and effectiveness, research operations, specific clinical procedures, and educational functions. The chapter provides guidelines for establishing requisites for the development and selection of an adequate information system, dissemination of information, and application of relevant knowledge. Finally, the implications of information management systems for the field of social work are reviewed.

BASIC REQUISITES

In designing an information system, the first requisite is its compatibility with other systems. Compatibility among systems increases their utility. For example, client needs in mental health agencies might be compared with those of clients in family service agencies. A yearly evaluation of an information management system is useful in determining how professionals use the system, what types of information are collected, and how the organization is structured to facilitate the use of data.

An agency must address the following questions: What types of data are needed? What kind of software is required? What forms are required to collect this data? Who collects the data? How are the data stored? How is the confidentiality of the data to be ensured? Is a data specialist needed? How can it be ensured that the appropriate individuals are involved in setting up the system and in its subsequent use?

The data to be collected in human service agencies include client traits, worker characteristics, intervention characteristics, and client outcomes. Such data enable managers to examine, for example, how many clients were served, who provided services, what types of services were provided, and how many times clients were seen. These data enhance an agency's ability to conduct cost-benefit analysis in order to determine the cost of a particular service relative to the outcomes achieved within a particular period of time. For example, an agency might determine that providing psychoeducation in addition to cognitive behavior therapy results in better outcomes within 3 months for clients with depression than either intervention alone does. An information system should prove invaluable to the assessment of a client, evaluation of services, documentation of intervention, and follow-up.

Individuals developing the data system must determine how many files should be free-form in contrast to fixed-form format. Free-form records are used to document client assessments, treatment, and follow-up. These records include open-ended questions, and clinicians can respond to items in a narrative format. Such records are rich in descriptive information; however, they are difficult to condense and summarize. For example, a team of researchers at the University at Albany partnered with two residential treatment centers to evaluate the effectiveness of their services. The social workers within the agency were primarily using progress notes to document the services provided. Members of the research team spent months reading and analyzing the narrative progress note entries to document the services social workers were providing to clients. The agencies are now implementing a new format for progress notes that includes a checklist of all services social workers provide to clients in the agency. This is a fixed-form record that allows for examining much more quickly the services workers are providing. Rather than reading through pages of progress notes, an information management system can quickly run a report that indicates which services were provided to clients during a 3-month period.

As in the example described above, a fixed-form record specifies the exact nature of the data to be collected. A typical example would be a structured interview schedule or questionnaire that includes fixed response categories. Information management systems allow practitioners to quickly summarize the number of clients who received services during a particular period by demographic characteristics, such as age, income, marital status, and number of children. The potential disadvantage of fixed-form records is that workers do not have the opportunity to indicate when one of the fixed responses does not adequately describe the client or the services provided. For example, a fixed-form interview question may ask whether the client has difficulty sleeping and provide two response categories, "yes" and "no." The client may indicate that he or she had difficulty sleeping until 2 weeks ago, when his or her doctor prescribed a sleep aid. This descriptive information may be important but is not captured in the fixed responses. One means of preventing this problem is to include fixed-response categories but also include a space for the worker to write free-form comments.

Before an agency sets up an information management system, it should involve as many workers as possible to enlist their support for the system's utilization. This allows for concerns to be addressed before the system is implemented. This involvement of staff should take place at the earliest possible date. Joint decisions should be made regarding the types of records needed. In the example described above, the research team worked closely with social workers, supervisors, and administrators to determine how the checklist should be completed by workers, how many services should be included in the checklist, and the appropriate terminology for each service. Because the workers are part of the planning process, future misunderstandings about how the checklist should be completed and about the terminology may be avoided. This planning process can also address typical concerns that record keeping will become more labor intensive. The planning process may need to include reducing other forms of record keeping as new responsibilities are added. For example, social workers may be instructed to write shorter narrative progress notes if they are being asked to complete a new checklist or questionnaire so that the total amount of time spent on record keeping will not increase.

MANAGERIAL APPLICATIONS

The applications of information technology address a wide range of problems and administrative tasks. One major area of application in the delivery of services is information management. Agencies are finding information management systems to be tremendous time savers in compiling service statistics, processing payrolls, and preparing financial reports. Moreover, these systems for managing data make possible forms of inquiry that were previously inconceivable, particularly because they permit more timely and expeditious use of sophisticated research techniques on routinely collected data.

DESCRIPTIVE ANALYSES

All agencies require descriptive data to document whom they have served and how. These data provide a rationale for the agency budget and help in planning for future needs. With appropriate intake forms, information is quickly and accurately gathered to determine (a) client characteristics, (b) duration of service, (c) cost of services, (d) provider characteristics, (e) follow-up results, and (f) additional services provided. Thus, an agency can benefit from knowing who its clients are and using these data in approaching the sources of support and gaining sanctions to extend the life of an agency. Once such a system is functional, an agency can conduct several cost-effectiveness analyses. This accountability requisite provides agencies with a means of deciding to alter, maintain, or expand services.

DIAGNOSIS, TREATMENT PLANNING, AND DOCUMENTATION OF PROGRAM IMPLEMENTATION AND EFFECTIVENESS

In addition to information management systems, agencies now have access to computerized questionnaires that may be administered and scored on agency computers. Workers then can generate reports from the data. The following are examples of questionnaires that have computerized versions.

Child Behavior Checklist (CBCL)

The purpose of the CBCL is to obtain ratings of a child's behavior from the child, parents, or other individuals—such as teachers—who know the child well. This instrument can either be self-administered or administered through an interview. The CBCL is available in a computerized format that allows practitioners to enter and score data as well as compare data obtained from parents, teachers, and children. The computerized version also facilitates measuring a child's change in behavior over time (Achenbach & Ruffle, 2000).

Millon Clinical Multiaxial Inventory–III (MCMI–III)

The MCMI–III is a personality assessment consistent with the *Diagnostic and Statistical Manual*. The program produces an interpretive report that assists practitioners in assessing personality characteristics and clinical disorders. In addition, the report includes a treatment guide, which provides the practitioners with treatment options based on the client's profile (Millon, Davis, Millon, & Grossman, 2006).

Minnesota Multiphasic Personality Inventory–II (MMPI–II)

The MMPI is a widely used assessment of personality characteristics that can be applied to detect symptoms of social and personal maladjustment. It has been used in correctional and criminal justice settings. The MMPI–II is the revised version. It is a lengthy assessment that includes 567 items and takes about 60 to 90 minutes to complete. The short version of the scale includes 370 items (Butcher, Dahlstrom, Graham, Tellegen, & Kaemmer, 2001; Pomeroy, Holleran, & Franklin, 2003).

Outcome Questionnaire

The Outcome Questionnaire is available in multiple versions and measures change in client symptoms and outcomes. Specifically, it measures functioning in three domains:

symptom distress, interpersonal functioning, and social role (Lambert et al., 1996). The Outcome Questionnaire–45.2 is a 45-item version of the questionnaire, but 30-item and 10-item versions also are available. There is also a parent version that allows parents to report about the behaviors of their children and adolescents.

Many personalized computer systems now aid in the administration of more than 50 assessment inventories. These can provide a wealth of information on which clinicians can base their assessment of the client and plan subsequent treatment (Hedlund, Vieweg, & Cho, 1985). Table 10.1 lists other available computerized measures.

The amount of information provided by these assessments is instrumental in promoting the use of evidence-based practice (Hudson, 1992; Wodarski, 1986). Because agencies

TABLE 10.1   Other Computerized Measures
Adjective Checklist
Bender Visual Motor Gestalt Test
California Psychological Inventory
Career Assessment Inventory
The Child Behavior Checklist
Clinical Analysis Questionnaire
The Exner Report for the Rorschach Comprehensive System
General Aptitude Test Battery
Giannetti Online Psychosocial History
Guilford-Zimmerman Temperament Survey
Hogan Personality Inventory
Millon Adolescent Personality Inventory – Clinical
Millon Adolescent Personality Inventory – Guidance
Millon Behavioral Health Inventory
Millon Clinical Multiaxial Inventory (MCMI)
Minnesota Multiphasic Personality Inventory (MMPI)
Multidimensional Personality Questionnaire
Myers-Briggs Type Indicator
Outcome Questionnaire (OQ)
The Rorschach Comprehensive System
Self-Description Inventory
Sixteen Personality Factors Questionnaire
Strong-Campbell Interest Inventory
Temperament and Values Inventory
Vocational Information Profile
Word and Number Assessment Inventory

often struggle to find the time and resources to rigorously evaluate their services, tools that make this process more efficient are essential for building capacity for evidence-based practice. On the other hand, relying on a computer-generated report of client characteristics and symptoms can seem impersonal, and there is little data on the reliability and validity of such reports (Springer & Franklin, 2003). Thus, social workers will need to use their professional judgment in integrating the data from these reports with other sources of evidence, such as feedback from clients and progress toward reaching treatment goals.

PRACTICE PROCEDURES THAT CAN BE COMPUTERIZED

In addition to streamlining the assessment process, practitioners can use information management systems to list goals, make progress notes, specify an intervention plan, and produce a timetable. Securing the documentation necessary to determine if goals have been met and subsequently analyzing the data with respect to meeting legal and administrative requisites is possible.

Numerous concrete items are easily computerized regardless of the practice context. Contracts formulated between clients and workers can be checked for the inclusion of the following: purposes of the interaction, targeted problems and areas of difficulties to be worked on, various goals and objectives to be accomplished, client and therapist duties, delineation of administrative procedures, techniques to be used, duration of contracts and criteria for termination, and renegotiation procedures.

Agencies can use goal-setting forms that specify a client's problem, plans for therapy, short- and long-term goals, plans for termination, follow-up procedures, and so forth. These forms facilitate the evaluation of clients' progress in meeting their treatment goals. Additionally, a summary form specifies the overall treatment plan, including termination and follow-up procedures. Access to this documentation should improve the services offered to clients.

Other computer functions to improve evaluation include checking to see if practice notes summarizing the major events of the client's latest visit are recorded within a reasonable time, such as 72 hours after the session, and determining if the follow-up visits are executed when necessary and placed in the client's record within a reasonable time. Also to be included are letters to all third parties regarding treatment plans and diagnosis, summary termination notes and follow-up procedures, and, if necessary, a letter to the referring professional or family doctor regarding the termination of services—all within 1 week of closing a case. In all instances, the energy and the time necessary to complete the forms should be kept to a minimum. Computers facilitate the execution of these requisite clinical tasks by simplifying the record-keeping process.

The use of information management systems in child welfare services provides an illustration of some of the benefits of these systems, as they have begun to play an important role in supporting assessment and decision making (Weaver, Moses, Furman, & Lindsey, 2003). These systems have reduced the need for manual recording of information and have streamlined the process of collecting and analyzing data. One example of the increased efficiency that results from the use of information management systems involves the former practice of examining the physical file of every child to provide an overview of the status of each case served by the Los Angeles County Department of Children and Family Services. The process typically required 80 hours of work from 24 staff members. Using the Child Welfare Services/Case Management System, departmental staff members have developed a reporting system that takes only 8 staff hours to accomplish the same task. As a result, this process, which used to be completed annually, can be completed monthly (Nguyen, 2007). Due to the more consistent use of data management systems, national data are now available on foster care and adoptions through the Adoptions and Foster Care Reporting and Analysis System and the National Data Analysis System (Nguyen, 2007).

RESEARCH OPERATIONS

For research, information management systems are essential. Once information is organized and entered into the computer, complicated calculations become routine. Transformation of data, simple graphing of client goals, and modification of data for further analysis are made easier. The accessibility of statistical software, such as SPSS, increases the capability of practitioners to execute basic statistical analyses on their cases. Thus, the ability to analyze different practice phenomena is enhanced. However, as with all technology, an adequate conceptual plan should guide the selection of appropriate analyses.

In summary, information management systems can assist human service workers in attaining the following clinical research goals:

1. Administration and scoring of tests

2. Interpretation and reporting

   a. Wechsler
   b. Rorschach
   c. MMPI

3. Client program planning and evaluation

   a. Goals
   b. Case progress
   c. Intervention plan
   d. Timetable

4. Program documentation

   a. Data recording and illustration
   b. Data analysis
   c. Attainment of legal and administrative requisites

5. Research applications

   a. Client progress
   b. Calculations
   c. Transformation of data
   d. Graphing client and administrative variables
   e. Updating information in a database

INFORMATIONAL REQUISITES

The first requisite in developing an information management system is to determine how the data will be collected and which forms are necessary. It is essential that the collected data be reliable and valid.

Second, it is essential that the agency consider the number of files that will be necessary for the collection of these data. The more files needed, the more complicated and costly an information management system becomes. The files also should be evaluated for how much data they will contain, how they will interface with other systems, and whether the central processing unit can handle the numbers.

SELECTING AN INFORMATION MANAGEMENT SYSTEM

The design of an information management system entails specifying an agency's needs and the purpose of the system. An assessment of financial and time resources is the next step, followed by a review of an agency's needs and resources by others knowledgeable about information systems. If available, a number of different management systems should be studied.

Second, consult various experts and others working with the system to see what they are doing with it. Visit a similar agency in which an information system is already operational; pilot test the system before full-scale implementation. Read journals that have sections devoted to the latest computer applications for human service agencies (e.g., *The Behavior Therapist,* by the Association of the Advancement of Behavior Therapy and Behavioral Assessment). Finally, after selection and implementation, annual review of the system is necessary to make modifications and improvements as needed.

The problem of knowledge utilization can be seen as an adoption problem related to the issue of training practitioners to search for and evaluate research data when choosing intervention alternatives. In certain cases, practitioners may be capable of conducting their own evaluations, but in most cases, they must rely on information and conclusions reported by more qualified professional researchers and evaluators. Certainly, social workers should be trained to monitor personally the effects of their interventions and to gather feedback on the direction and magnitude of change, interpret studies for their relevance, and implement time-series designs. But workers rarely possess the resources and skills of a professional evaluator, which may be necessary to perform a summary evaluation of the effects of a program or change strategy.

Research indicates that certain characteristics of practitioners and of the new technologies predict whether practitioners will use them. Perceived self-efficacy for using the technology; perceived benefits of using the technology; and use of incentives, such as recognition and monetary rewards, are associated with better rates of new practice adoption among practitioners. In addition, technologies that are easier to learn and use are more readily adopted than those that require specialized skills (Carrilio, 2007; Corrigan, Steiner, McCracken, Blaser, & Barr, 2001; Franklin & Hopson, 2007). To ensure that professionals keep abreast of current treatment developments, and that they will implement them, the incentive structure of social work practice must be changed: social workers will have to be rewarded.

ISSUES FOR THE FIELD

Even if information management systems become readily available and agencies implement them, technical expertise will be necessary to aid in the interpretation and summarization of the knowledge they produce. Moreover, experts should be prepared to summarize the data and disseminate them to other agencies that deal with similar clients. This process will add to the knowledge base of service providers. In the absence of such integration, chaos may ensue. Second, yearly evaluations are required to update a data system as needed. Sufficient time should be spent in setting up an adequate system, since it is much more difficult and costly to change a data system once it is operational. Third, the human service field must come to grips with defining outcomes and standards for service. When outcomes are ambiguous, standardizing them is impossible and comparisons across agencies are meaningless.

Information systems can be utilized to plan and implement agency goals. For example, computers can (a) facilitate an empirical approach to the identification, collection, organization, and analysis of data and information about clients; (b) aid in the study of the component processes and outcomes of human service delivery systems; (c) clarify the state of human service needs and how practitioners can facilitate the strengths of clients; (d) aid in practitioners' learning theories and practicing various skills; and (e) facilitate the evaluation of different theories of behavioral change and intervention.

In essence, for informational management systems to facilitate the provision of relevant services to clients, the following recommendations are proposed: the field should develop standards for practice; data management systems should be developed so human service agencies can interact with one another, such as mental health interfacing with criminal justice and child welfare programs; and, at the national level, a data system might be developed that would lead to the identification of how social policies of both federal and state governments affect clients.

The client change process and the interventions used to help clients are complex. Computers can facilitate an understanding of these processes and, thus, enhance a practitioner's ability to tailor appropriate interventions built on a client's strengths.

Questions for Discussion

A community-based agency providing multiple services to children and families—including mental health services, case management, and family preservation services—introduces a new information management system.

1. What are some potential advantages of using such a system in this agency?

2. What are some likely obstacles that could prevent the system from being used effectively by clinicians? How could these obstacles be addressed?

3. What are some ethical concerns in implementing this system? How would you address or prevent these concerns?

4. How could information from the system be used to improve clinical supervision?

References

Achenbach, T. M., & Ruffle, T. M. (2000). The Child Behavior Checklist and related forms for assessing behavioral/emotional problems and competencies. *Pediatrics in Review, 21,* 265–271.

Butcher, J. N., Dahlstrom, W. G., Graham, J. R., Tellegen, A., & Kaemmer, B. (2001). *MMPI-2 (Minnesota Multiphasic Personality Inventory 2): Manual for administration and scoring* (Rev. ed.). Minneapolis: University of Minnesota Press.

Carrilio, T. E. (2007). Using client information systems in practice settings: Factors affecting social workers' use of information systems. *Journal of Technology in the Human Services, 25*(4), 41–62.

Corrigan, P. W., Steiner, L., McCracken, S. G., Blaser, B., & Barr, M. (2001). Strategies for disseminating evidence-based practices to staff who treat people with serious mental illness. *Psychiatric Services, 52,* 1598–1606.

Franklin, C., & Hopson, L. (2007). Facilitating the use of evidence-based practice in community organizations. *Journal of Social Work Education, 43*(3), 377–404.

Hedlund, J. L., Vieweg, B. W., & Cho, D. W. (1985). Mental health computing in the 1980s: I. General information systems and clinical documentation. *Computers in Human Services. 1,* 3–33.

Hudson, W. W. (1992). *The WALMYR assessment scales scoring manual.* Tempe, AZ: WALMYR.

Lambert, M. J., Burlingame, G. M., Umphress, V., Hansen, N. B., Vermeersch, D. A., Clouse, G. C., et al. (1996). The reliability and validity of the Outcome Questionnaire. *Clinical Psychology and Psychotherapy, 3,* 249–258.

Millon, T., Davis, R., Millon, C., & Grossman, S. (2006). *The Millon Clinical Multiaxial Inventory–III* (3rd ed.). Port Jervis, NY: Institute for Advanced Studies in Personality and Psychopathology. Retrieved February 4, 2009, from http://millon.net/instruments/MCMI_III.htm

Nguyen, L. H. (2007). Child welfare informatics: A new definition for an established practice. *Social Work, 52*(4), 361–363.

Pomeroy, E. C., Holleran, L., & Franklin, C. (2003). Chapter 7: Adults. In C. Jordan & C. Franklin (Eds.), *Clinical assessment for social work: Quantitative and qualitative methods.* Chicago: Lyceum.

Springer, D., & Franklin, C. (2003). Standardized assessment measures and computer-assisted assessment technologies. In C. Jordan & C. Franklin (Eds.), *Clinical assessment for social workers: Qualitative and quantitative methods* (2nd ed., pp. 97–137). Chicago: Lyceum.

Weaver, D., Moses, T., Furman, W., & Lindsey, D. (2003). The effects of computerization on public child welfare practice. *Journal of Social Service Research, 29,* 67–80.

Wodarski, J. S. (1986). The application of computer technology to enhance the effectiveness of family therapy. *Family Therapy, 13,* 5–13.

Developing and Formulating Quality Proposals

Researchers often need to secure support for their activities. Social science research needs support in its attempt to answer complex and difficult questions. Such studies require large amounts of energy and resources. This chapter reviews the basics of securing support.

INFORMATIONAL EXCHANGE

All research proposals, whether for federal and state agencies, private foundations, or business and industry, have similarities. They require clearly specified aims that align with the funder's mission, strong methodological procedures appropriate for the research questions, and experienced investigators. The basic differences between the requirements of the various funding sources are the length of the proposal and the approach. Proposals to federal agencies usually are the most lengthy. State agencies, private foundations, and business and industry usually require a shorter proposal and the development of a relationship between someone at the university and an individual within the agency.

Many grant proposals fail because certain issues are not addressed by those formulating the grant. If the research proponent spends enough time dealing with these issues, succeeding in getting a proposal funded is highly probable. As the purpose of grants is to solve significant problems, it is up to the researcher to identify such problems and convince a review panel that the allocation of funds will contribute significantly to the solution of those problems. Each proponent has to develop sources of available grants. This will mean attending conferences and maintaining contacts with state and federal agencies, foundations, and business concerns. If such contacts are maintained, up-to-date information can be provided to facilitate a competitive grant proposal (Coley & Scheinberg, 2007; Wodarski, 1990).

KNOWLEDGE

It is essential for a prospective researcher to know the objectives and foci of the granting agency and to tailor the proposal to meet the specific needs of the agency—that is, faculty needs should match funding source interests. How the proposal addresses the major concerns of the agency should be elaborated through a relevant, clear, and concise review of the literature (Locke, Spirduso, & Silverman, 2007). Often, an organization will provide a description of its funding priorities, as well as a list of currently funded projects, on its website. Agency publications, such as annual reports, are also important sources.

PERSONAL CONTACTS

Before formulating a proposal, the applicant should contact an agency representative to learn what the agency needs. For federal and state agencies, this usually requires a telephone call. For private foundations, a brief letter outlining the project is sufficient. For business and industry, a phone call is also necessary. Introductions to key individuals are essential for state, industrial, and private foundation funds. For example, working with foundations is eased if a faculty member can secure an endorsement. For university researchers, good working relationships between university research office personnel or department heads and agency representatives also help secure a grant.

Before contacting a funding agency, the principal investigator must isolate the following concerns: Is the research idea central to the agency's mission? Is the potential researcher on the cutting edge of research and theoretical development in that area? Is the researcher competent in the methodological and theoretical issues that face the field? Whether the agency wishes to be approached by telephone or letter must be ascertained. A 5-minute telephone conversation with an agency official to determine the agency's interest in an idea can save a principal investigator many months of hard work. The agency official can highlight the aspects of a proposal that are consistent with the agency's funding priorities. Conversely, this brief conversation can clearly communicate that the proposal is inconsistent with these priorities. The researcher can then decide whether the proposal needs to be revised or whether there may be other, more appropriate funding sources for the existing proposal.

Before the telephone contact is made, researchers should practice delivering the central ideas of the proposal and how they will approach the idea. They should also formulate specific questions concerning the agency's focus. If the contact indicates that the idea is mutually beneficial, the researcher should ask whether the agency would like to review a brief concept paper. The characteristics of effective concept papers are described in greater detail next. The proposal should be reviewed by other colleagues before it is forwarded to the funding agency. When an agency does not solicit telephone calls but will accept a letter, usually the same procedures as outlined above will apply. Written material from the agency can serve as a guide.

CONCEPT PAPERS

The concept paper must elucidate the general need addressed by the proposal, and it should include a specific demonstration of the researcher's knowledge in the area and his or her competencies with theoretical and methodological issues. Every word in this concept paper is important. The investigator must be concise; ambiguous statements must be clarified. It is necessary to be as succinct as possible in the concept paper. Some funders require a letter of inquiry that serves a similar function. Concept papers provide an overview of the proposed research and include enough detail about the research questions, design, methods, and analyses for reviewers to make an initial assessment about whether the research is appropriate, given the mission and research expectations of the funding organization. The paper should elucidate the investigator's intentions to address the agency's needs through a relevant methodology. In some instances, agency personnel will consent to review a total proposal before it is submitted. Investigators should capitalize on such offers and incorporate relevant suggestions into the final proposal.

Many agencies have prefunding conferences. If the topics are of interest to the researcher, he or she should definitely plan to attend. At these conferences, agencies explain the objectives of their programs and how grant proposals are to be prepared. Conferences also are invaluable for making contact with key agency personnel to facilitate the submission of competitive proposals.

KEY CONTACT PERSONS

Foundations and businesses typically require that a key contact be provided for an individual wishing to formulate a proposal. After making contact with the agency, the researcher must determine the agency's interest in reviewing a proposal. It is possible the agency is interested only in inflating the number of applications received. Foundations may be more likely to fund a proposal from a researcher with whom they have a relationship.

DEVELOPING A PROPOSAL

Obtaining critiques from colleagues is essential when developing a proposal. These critiques will facilitate a clearer writing style and will foster creativity in addressing theoretical and methodological issues.

As the development of the proposal proceeds, the investigator must feel free to call the agency for consultation. Program managers are more than willing to assist an individual in formulating a proposal with the latest research findings and outcome measures. Moreover, grant administrators desire contact with individuals in the field. After all, agencies must fund proposals to stay in business. The proposals should outline the issue to address, the methodology to use, the tasks the proposal seeks to perform, the staff members who will perform the tasks, and a timetable to follow for the performance of these tasks. The online resources provided at the end of this chapter provide useful advice for preparing grant applications.

Reviewers of a grant proposal must be convinced that the researcher has the capacity to implement the proposed research. Review boards are composed primarily of individuals who have written many proposals, and these individuals evaluate the quality as well as the feasibility of the proposed research. Choosing a co-principal investigator who complements the principal investigator is often helpful. Federal agencies focus on proposals of an interdisciplinary nature because of the complexity of theoretical knowledge of the world.

Do not bluff! Review committee members have many proposals to read. There is nothing as disturbing as reading an endless proposal by an individual who is evidently not knowledgeable about the subject. Grant committees are composed of experts who usually meet to review and assign scores to proposals. Reviewers are knowledgeable, busy individuals who become frustrated with poorly organized proposals. Because reviewers are able to spend little time reviewing any one application, the application must clearly and concisely communicate the purpose of the research and its significance. Review members will evaluate the researcher's grasp of a topic by examining whether key research is cited in the proposal and whether the researcher has a track record, evidenced by articles published in recognized scholarly journals. They may also want to know that the researcher has received funding in the past. Budgets should be prepared with particular care because all reviewers have extensive budget experience; thus, it pays to justify relevant budget items. Moreover, to help in the general comprehension of ideas, a proposal should be executed with accurate typing, clear copies, and a definitive organizational style.

CRITERIA FOR EVALUATION

Reviewers typically will be evaluating research proposals based on the following criteria:

- Quality of writing and logical presentation of ideas

- Consistency of the research with the funder's mission and interests

- Rigorous methods consistent with the goals and objectives of the proposal

- Culturally appropriate methods and recruitment procedures that provide adequate representation by gender, race, and ethnicity

- Feasibility of the proposed research given the amount of funding requested and the researcher's expertise

- Scientific relevance, or the extent to which the proposed research is likely to contribute to the scientific knowledge base in a particular area

- Availability and discussion of pilot data that clearly support the proposed research

- The expertise and research experience of the researcher

- The size and prestige of the research facility in which the research is to be conducted

Providing justification for the proposed methods is important because reviewers have expertise in assessing whether the research designs and methods are appropriate for addressing the goals and objectives. Make a convincing case that your proposed design and methods would provide strong evidence related to your research questions. Acknowledging the limitations of the research methods is also important. Researchers should demonstrate that they have thought through the implications of the limitations and have made attempts to minimize their impact on the internal validity of the study.

FOLLOW-UP

No news from the agency concerning a submitted proposal is usually good news. However, it is acceptable to place a follow-up telephone call to check on the status of the proposal's review after the notification date has expired.

RESUBMISSION OF THE PROPOSAL

When a proposal is not funded, many agencies provide evaluation sheets that indicate the strengths and limitations of the proposal and suggestions for improvement. If the methodological and theoretical issues outlined on the evaluation sheet are addressed, the probability of the grant applicant receiving funding for the revised proposal is extremely high. An investigator should address the evaluation sheet issues individually. Moreover, agencies prefer that investigators specify how a revised proposal has incorporated issues contained in the evaluation sheets. This is usually achieved through a cover letter. Aspects of the proposal that have been changed in response to a reviewer's comments should be highlighted. One fatal mistake is assuming that a proposal will never be funded if it does not receive a positive, constructive critique. A proposal must be submitted to be funded.

TIPS FOR OBTAINING RESEARCH GRANTS

The following tips have helped in grant-proposal preparation:

1. Cultivate relationships with key staff members in foundations and governmental agencies that offer research grant funds. Personal contact nurtured by correspondence, telephone conversations, and, most desirably, in-person meetings with the contact at conferences or in his or her office are indispensable for obtaining guidance, advice, and feedback on all steps in the grant-application process.

2. Find out which research areas are "hot" and timely through colleagues who are successful grant recipients and through agency contacts. Drug abuse and child abuse have become popular research areas in recent years. As the population continues to age, geriatric research will become more popular. Interdisciplinary research that addresses social problems also has become a priority for many funding agencies.

3. With the active collaboration of a knowledgeable and helpful staff person, develop the proposal in steps: (a) concept paper, (b) preliminary proposal, and (c) final draft. Actively solicit input and feedback.

4. Develop local support as the proposal is formulated. Do not wait until after the application has been forwarded to obtain the "blessings" of administrators, collaborators, and consultants. Cost-sharing agreements are particularly attractive to granting agencies.

5. Know who on the review committee will evaluate and judge the application. This may help the researcher "tailor" aspects of the design and method. Citing grant reviewers' research may result in a more favorable review.

6. Write detailed and explicit justifications for all budget items, especially when outlining tasks, roles, and time involvement for each individual listed in the "personnel" category.

7. Write a focused and objectively balanced "background" section. This should be a scholarly, but not encyclopedic, review of literature pertinent and relevant to the proposed research. Keep interpretation and opinion to a minimum in this section, saving interpretive comments for the "rationale" and "significance" sections.

8. Write the "methods" section clearly and cogently because it is the critical segment of the application. Visual aids are a must to facilitate the reviewers' comprehension of main ideas. Include flow charts, timetables, figures, and tables to help the reviewers "see" exactly what is planned. For example, a table showing how dependent variables are organized to measure the anticipated effects of a treatment intervention conveys the investigator's grasp of the project.

9. Whenever possible in treatment research, specify what intervention will be presented, how therapists will be trained, what criteria of competency will be used, and how the therapy will be carried out with clients and patients. For example, the existence of a written treatment manual and criteria for evaluating the competence of therapists are assets to a grant application. Also helpful is a description of how the investigators will monitor the fidelity of the therapists and therapy to the treatment methods and concepts.

10. Consider whether the training and experience level of the therapists are appropriate for the demands of the methods and target population.

11. Keep project application design simple, and limit the number of hypotheses and questions being asked of the data. Be modest in prioritizing specific aims and objectives, acknowledging the limitations of the available subject pool (i.e., the "N"), the time to do the project, and the quality and quantity of data.

12. Consultants are valuable for what they will tangibly offer the project and for their reputation in the field. Consultants will need to have a solid track record for conducting research in an area related to the proposed research. It is often helpful to include as a consultant someone who has been funded by the targeted funding agency in the past.

13. Keep the text terse, neutral, tight, and free of jargon and biases. Write for the intelligent layman as well as for the fellow researchers; this achieves a proper balance. In order to accomplish this, it is helpful to request that the proposal be reviewed by someone who is not a researcher to determine whether the concepts and goals of the research are clear. The reviewers rarely are as familiar with the area of research as the investigator, and the proposal will not receive favorable reactions if the material cannot be understood.

14. The investigator should try to arrange a site visit in order to more fully inform the review committee of plans and competence before the proposal is finally evaluated.

15. View grant writing as a learning experience, utilizing modeling and "trial-and-error" processes. Rarely will a novice receive a research grant award on a first try, but revisions and resubmissions based on review committee and staff feedback will yield positive results in the hands of a persistent researcher.

Overview

The basics of preparing a quality proposal have been explained in this chapter. It should be emphasized that developing a quality proposal requires substantial time and energy. The probability of securing funds increases when research activities are aimed toward the solution of a significant problem society faces. To get funding, the researcher must prepare many proposals and resubmit rejected proposals. The difficulty should not be underestimated, but the rewards are substantial.

Questions for Discussion

1. What are some preliminary steps that are important in preparing a grant for submission?

2. What are some advantages of submitting a concept paper?

3. What are some of the main criteria reviewers will use to determine whether to fund a proposal?

4. How can you increase the likelihood that a proposal will be funded?

Online Funding Resources

Grants.gov

This site provides information about U.S. federal agencies that manage grant funds and available funding mechanisms.

NIH Research Portfolio Online Reporting Tools (RePORT), http://projectreporter.nih.gov/reporter.cfm

RePORT is a searchable database of information on federally funded research projects.

National Institutes of Health Guide for Grants and Contracts, http://grants.nih.gov/grants/guide/

This site provides information about grant opportunities available through the National Institutes of Health, as well as information on grant policies.

National Institutes of Health, http://www.nlm.nih.gov/ep/Tutorial.html

This site provides tutorials on preparing grants for the National Institutes of Health.

The Foundation Center, http://foundationcenter.org

This site provides a directory of private grant-funding organizations.

Substance Abuse and Mental Health Services Administration (SAMHSA), http://www.samhsa.gov/samhsanewsletter/Volume_17_Number_5/WinningGrantProposal.aspx

This site provides advice on preparing a grant proposal for SAMHSA.

National Science Foundation, http://www.nsf.gov/pubs/gpg/nsf04_23/index.jsp

This site provides advice on preparing a grant proposal for the National Science Foundation.

John D. and Katharine T. MacArthur Foundation, http://www.macfound.org/site/c.lkLXJ8MQKrH/b.913959/k.E1BE/Applying_for_Grants.htm

This site provides advice on preparing a grant proposal.

U.S. Department of Education, http://www2.ed.gov/about/offices/list/ocfo/grants/grants.html

This site provides advice on preparing a grant and opportunities with the Department of Education.

References

Coley, S. M., & Scheinberg, C. A. (2007). *Proposal writing: Effective grantsmanship.* (3rd ed.). Thousand Oaks, CA: Sage.

Locke, L. F., Spirduso, W. W., & Silverman, S. J. (2007). *Proposals that work: A guide for planning dissertations and grant proposals* (5th ed.). Thousand Oaks, CA: Sage.

Wodarski, J. S. (1990). *The university research enterprise.* Springfield, IL: Charles C Thomas.

CHAPTER 12

Emerging Trends and Issues Related to Evidence-Based Practice

Chapters 1 and 2 discussed evidence-based practice as a process that involves the use of professional judgment in synthesizing information about research evidence and client needs. The following chapters reviewed the basic conceptual and methodological processes practitioners need to incorporate behavioral science knowledge and research in their repertoires for evaluating their practices. This chapter concludes this discussion of evidence-based practice by addressing the emerging trends and issues in social work practice research, including the relationship between researchers and practitioners, rapid assessment techniques, organizational aspects of research, and dissemination of research.

DISSEMINATION OF RESEARCH

If practitioners are to participate in practice research, which is a necessary condition in developing the treatment technology needed for the field, they will need the basic evidence-based practice skills, such as the ability to synthesize information in the research literature, formulate questions that will guide practice research, decide on various data options needed to answer the questions, and make rational decisions on the basis of data and the existing research literature. However, even if these skills are mastered, there are many challenges to implementing these skills.

One problem with the adoption of research-based interventions is a lack of effective communication between the practitioner and the evaluator (Bernstein & Freeman, 1975; Kettlewell, 2004). More information is needed about the informational mechanisms used by social workers before any progress can be made. Although researchers communicate through professional journals and meetings, practitioners likely do not rely heavily on these mechanisms. To reach the practitioner, advocates of research need to include knowledge of the informational mechanisms and informal networks of the practitioner in their studies, and possibly have the practitioner and researcher work on studies together for one solution and then make use of those studies to disseminate knowledge. For example, in the field of education, the change agent usually resides in the superintendent of schools or in other administrative positions. The research-evaluation work on innovative procedures and products usually is done in a university or research-and-development setting and reported in journal articles or technical reports, which are read by only a small minority of the school administrators. Administrators typically rely on reports from colleagues and on their own professional organizations and publications for information on new procedures and products. Researchers and evaluators in education are beginning to realize they must be able to supply their information through the channels used by administrators if they want their stories told.

It would be a mistake, however, to assume that the availability of good practice research information will automatically lead to improved services. The history of knowledge utilization in other human services fields shows clearly that the change process is much more complicated than implied by a simple linear model leading from production to utilization of knowledge. In fact, in most cases, the effective dissemination and use of new findings is as difficult as their production (Martinez-Brawley, 1995).

Research indicates that, although there are many well-researched interventions, few practitioners are using them in agency settings. Some of the reasons include insufficient funds and resources for implementing these interventions, inadequate training in prerequisite skills, practitioner burnout and large caseloads, and the belief that currently used practices are superior (Franklin & Hopson, 2007). Thus, to ensure that professionals will keep abreast of current treatment developments and, moreover, will implement them, it may be necessary to incentivize the adoption of evidence-based practice.

In addition to the challenges in accessing current research literature and implementing effective practices, certain challenges are inherent in evaluating practice in social services agencies. In some cases, practitioners may be capable of conducting their own evaluation, but in most cases, they must rely on information and conclusions reported by more qualified professional researchers or evaluators. Certainly, social workers should be trained to personally monitor the effects of their interventions and to gather feedback on the direction and magnitude of change, interpret studies for their relevance, and implement time-series designs. However, social workers rarely possess the resources and prerequisite training in evaluation skills required to perform a comprehensive evaluation of the reliable outcomes of a program or change strategy.

RESEARCHERS AND PRACTITIONERS

The division of research and practice has proven detrimental to practice research because one cannot effectively operate without feedback from the other. Detachment of professionals engaged only in research and those engaged only in practice precludes possible exchange of information needed for research of practice problems. However, this structural problem in social work is one not easily overcome. If the profession is to improve services offered to clients through use of research, there must be a substantial increase in the number of research practitioners who are able to operationalize social work practice goals and assess through collected data whether such goals have been attained. This means that professional development for social workers will need to synthesize training in practice skills with methods for evaluating practice. Rather than offering courses that teach social work students research methods and other courses that teach advanced practice skills, courses that provide content on advanced practice skills will need to include strategies for evaluating the effectiveness of those skills in practice settings.

THE RESEARCHERS' RELATIONSHIP WITH CLIENTS

Open lines of communication between the investigators and the population to be served will help ensure that research is relevant to client needs. This can be accomplished by (a) placing clients on the review boards of granting agencies, (b) hiring clients to conduct various aspects of the research, (c) having the empirical practitioner spend time with the clients in the clients' environment, and (d) training practitioners in research methodology relevant for evaluating their daily practice. For example, large sums of money are now being spent on research to improve the criminal justice system. However, unless researchers gain relevant input concerning client needs, their research endeavors may prove nonproductive. Surely one cannot expect significant studies to be designed in the ivory towers of university settings without the proper fieldwork.

PARTICIPATORY ACTION RESEARCH

Many researchers find benefits in close collaboration with both key personnel and the clients themselves in planning the research. Participatory Action Research (PAR) is an attractive methodology for researchers interested in involving community agencies and their target population at every phase of the research process. PAR involves collaboration between researchers and participants in developing goals and methods, data gathering and analysis, and implementing a change process that the participating group can direct or control (Kidd & Kral, 2005). PAR requires an openness on the researcher's part to using participants' definitions of their needs and potential solutions (Kidd & Kral, 2005) and shared power in making decisions at every phase of the research process (Kelly, 2005).

The researcher using PAR methods takes on the role of consultant and serves to facilitate rather than direct the research process (Gosin, Dustman, Drapeau, & Harthun, 2003). This can mean making compromises in implementation and evaluation strategies, because the researcher cannot necessarily impose the design that may be most rigorous if the clients or agency personnel indicate that such a design would be inappropriate. Conducting PAR does not mean, however, that the researcher is permitted to disregard issues of reliability and validity in the study design (Kidd & Kral, 2005). Including procedures to protect the methodological strength of the study is critical to ensure that time and money are not wasted in conducting an evaluation that will provide little reliable and valid information about outcomes. Because PAR studies typically do not employ experimental design methods but, rather, more qualitative methods and case studies, it is often more difficult to definitively demonstrate program effectiveness (Hughes, 2003).

Using PAR methods can be an effective means of incorporating the cultural and learning styles of participants and providing a sense of ownership in a new intervention (Gosin et al., 2003). For example, PAR methods were used in the development and evaluation of an evidence-based substance abuse prevention program called "keepin' it REAL." The curriculum was developed in collaboration with local youth and teachers, using focus groups and interviews to gather narratives about life experiences, substance use, and use of strategies to resist substance use, in addition to information about the school settings in which the curriculum was to be delivered. These narratives informed the content and structure of the curriculum, including the use of the four resistance strategies: refuse, explain, avoid, and leave (Gosin et al., 2003; Hecht et al., 2003). PAR methods employed during the development and evaluation of keepin' it REAL include the following:

- Interviews with middle school– and high school–age youth about their life experiences, substance use, and use of resistance strategies, which informed curriculum design

- Focus groups with teachers to evaluate the curriculum prior to implementation

- Focus groups with teachers to evaluate the curriculum following implementation

- Field testing the curriculum with students and obtaining student feedback

- Engaging youth in the creation of videos for the curriculum

- Maintaining ongoing contact and collaboration with facilitators during implementation

Using these methods helped ensure that the intervention captured the culture and life experiences of the target population. They strengthened the evaluation, as well, because the input of the target population and facilitators guided the implementation of methods that would be culturally appropriate and feasible within the participating school settings.

ADAPTATION OF EVIDENCE-BASED INTERVENTIONS

Many researchers assume that, unless an evidence-based curriculum is implemented with fidelity, its effectiveness will be greatly compromised. Yet few community settings, such as schools, have successfully implemented curricula with strict adherence to established protocols. Reasons for lack of program fidelity in the community include inadequate training and support, staff turnover, large classroom sizes, and insufficient resources. Evidence-based curricula are also likely to have been developed and tested with White, middle-class youth, whereas school settings typically serve students from many different ethnic and cultural backgrounds (Botvin, 2004).

Because interventions are seldom implemented with great fidelity in the community, researchers have begun to examine the benefits and consequences of adapting evidence-based curricula. Although adaptation may affect a program's effectiveness, it also allows community organizations to tailor an intervention to meet the needs of their particular population. Improving the fit between an intervention and a community organization can increase buy-in from staff and consumers and increase the likelihood that the organization will continue to use the intervention (Castro, Barrera, & Martinez, 2004). Research also indicates that culturally grounded adaptations of evidence-based programs improve recruitment and retention of participants (Kumpfer, Alvarado, Smith, & Bellamy, 2002).

For example, evidence-based prevention programs are perceived in many communities as inappropriate for local youth because they were developed and tested in a different community with samples not representative of their youth (Botvin, 2004; Castro et al., 2004). Facilitating an adaptation process to make evidence-based prevention more appropriate for a given community agency or school is one way to resolve this tension. Yet there is little existing research to guide the process of adaptation or to indicate whether an adapted program can be effective (Kumpfer et al., 2002).

The debate continues about whether adaptation should be encouraged and the types of adaptations that would be helpful (Botvin, 2004; Kumpfer et al., 2002). Research needs to explore means of adaptation that allow community organizations to personalize the curriculum without compromising the core components that make the intervention effective. Without this type of research, well-researched prevention programs will likely remain unused by social services agencies, and the programs will fail to reach the youth that need them most.

THE ORGANIZATIONAL CONTEXT FOR RESEARCH

Research is frequently based on the assumption that it takes place in a static, unchanging agency. Even when research meets all the requirements of a well-designed study, the researcher faces the problem of executing the study in real-world settings that may have high practitioner turnover, clients with multiple complex presenting problems, and large caseloads. These organizational characteristics, along with administrative styles, level of worker training, and number of years of experience, affect practice research. Procedures must be developed to evaluate the confounding effect of the organizational aspects of the agency where the research takes place. A minimal requisite of any research study is adequate specification of the characteristics of the organization in which the study was conducted to permit consumers of the research to determine the applicability of findings in their particular organizations. This knowledge will also provide clues to how organizational variables interact to affect worker behavior and, ultimately, client outcomes (Feldman & Wodarski, 1974; Glisson & James, 2002).

The organizational context also influences the use of research-based interventions. Constructive organizational cultures in which practitioners respect one another, work well together, and are encouraged to take on challenging tasks are more conducive to using new interventions. That practitioners and administrators perceive an intervention is consistent with organizational values is also important (Glisson & James, 2002; Miller, 2001). The organizational leadership is instrumental in creating an environment that supports the use of new, innovative practices (Franklin & Hopson, 2007; Gambrill, 2006).

In addition to influencing readiness to implement new interventions, the organizational environment can directly influence client outcomes. In a study of organizational climate and interagency collaboration, Glisson and Hemmelgarn (1998) found that an organizational climate characterized by low conflict and cooperation predicted higher-quality services and improved psychosocial functioning among children served by the agencies.

Thus, measuring organizational factors is important for understanding their impact on client outcomes, determining the feasibility of conducting an evaluation, and establishing an agency's readiness for adopting new interventions. A growing body of research is examining interventions designed to create an organizational context as the foundation for use of effective practices (Hemmelgarn, Glisson, & James, 2006).

RAPID ASSESSMENT INSTRUMENTS

As agencies are increasingly called on to demonstrate the effectiveness of their services, they are seeking more efficient means of assessing clients' needs and evaluating their progress toward reaching treatment goals (Hopson & Wodarski, 2008). Regardless of the quality of an intervention and its implementation, insufficient time spent on assessment results in ineffective or irrelevant intervention because the client's difficulties were not accurately assessed.

Rapid assessment instruments (RAIs) can build capacity for implementing evidence-based practice because they provide an efficient, often low-cost means of assessing clients and tracking their progress over time. RAIs are standardized questionnaires that require little time to complete and score. They are designed to provide ongoing feedback for the purposes of documenting client change during the helping process. This is important in current practice contexts. Practitioners in many agencies are more likely to use RAIs than more time-consuming measures due to the influence of managed-care policies (Cashel, 2002; Hopson & Wodarski, 2008; Wood, Garb, Lilienfield, & Nezworski, 2002). In addition, many managed-care organizations will reimburse only for a brief amount of time devoted to assessment.

A number of RAIs have been developed to facilitate obtaining the information necessary for workers to make adequate assessments of their clients (Rittner & Wodarski, 1995). Fischer and Corcoran (2007) identify more than 400 RAIs for use with individuals, couples, and families, to assess for a wide array of presenting problems. These RAIs are also in the public domain and, thus, do not require that social workers purchase them or obtain permission for using them with clients.

In addition to providing efficient means of assessment, RAIs increase the feasibility of evaluating interventions with clients. For example, practitioners can demonstrate the effectiveness of their interventions through single-case design studies in which they repeatedly administer an RAI to evaluate a client's progress toward reaching treatment goals (Hopson & Wodarski, 2008). Because they are reliable, quickly administered, and easily scored, practitioners can feasibly incorporate RAIs into their regular sessions with clients and assess for changes in scores over time.

TRAINING AND PROFESSIONAL DEVELOPMENT

Although practitioners and agencies are increasingly required to use evidence-based practices and systematically apply and evaluate these interventions, progress has been slow. Many agencies do not have the funds to train their practitioners in evidence-based practices. In addition, agencies with high staff turnover are reluctant to invest in trainings that demand agency time and resources, because trained practitioners may leave the agency (Franklin & Hopson, 2007).

Effective training in evidence-based practices is critical to ensuring they are used in social services agencies. The challenge lies in providing necessary training to practitioners, who have a range of training experiences and skill sets. Some practitioners within an agency may have received training in multiple evidence-based practices in their master's education programs or as continuing education, while other practitioners may have no formal training in interventions considered to be evidence based. Many social work master's programs do not provide training in evidence-based practices (Weissman et al., 2006). In addition, faculty widely vary in the level of research support they consider sufficient to deem an intervention evidence based (Rubin & Parrish, 2007). According to a survey of 64 randomly selected social work master's programs, less than half reported providing training in evidence-based practices using the most effective training practices, which include ongoing supervision and consultation (Weissman et al., 2006). The result is a workforce with diverse training needs and limited expertise in evidence-based interventions.

Community-based training models are often inadequate for promoting and sustaining the use of evidence-based practices as well. Even when an agency offers training to all clinicians, they may not attend the entire training and there is no guarantee that trained clinicians will use the newly learned intervention with clients (Corrigan, Steiner, McCracken, Blaser, & Barr, 2001). Research indicates that practitioners are most likely to acquire new skills when they are provided with trainings that include ongoing consultation and technical assistance. The traditional 2-day intensive training in a particular intervention is less likely to result in effective implementation than training models that provide ongoing access to trainers or curriculum developers so that practitioners can ask questions and receive assistance with implementation (Franklin & Hopson, 2007).

Many evidence-based practices include easy-to-follow training manuals and require no specialized training. However, even these interventions typically require some basic skills in cognitive or behavioral techniques (Franklin & Hopson, 2007). Practitioners have varying levels of expertise in these techniques. Those who have experience and training in these basic skills may have greater success in implementing new practices because research indicates that perceived self-efficacy in implementing a new practice is associated with adopting that practice (Corrigan et al., 2001; Rohrbach, Grana, Sussman, & Valente, 2006; Schoenwald & Hoagwood, 2001).

Overview

This chapter has discussed emerging trends related to evidence-based practice. Even if social workers are trained in the steps of implementing evidence-based practice, many challenges are involved in applying these steps in community settings. These challenges include a need for more resources; better collaboration among researchers, practitioners, and clients; improved training models; and more culturally relevant interventions. Some promising strategies for addressing these challenges include PAR methods; culturally grounded adaptations of evidence-based interventions; and cost-effective measurement tools, such as RAIs, that make evaluation more feasible for agencies.

Questions for Discussion

1. Describe some barriers to dissemination of research into practice settings. What are some strategies for facilitating dissemination?

2. Compare a PAR approach with more traditional research approaches to (a) the research question(s), (b) the research design, (c) measures used, and (d) data analysis. What are the strengths and limitations of using PAR?

3. Explain how RAIs can promote the use of evidence-based practice.

References

Bernstein, I. N., & Freeman, H. E. (1975). *Academic and entrepreneurial research.* New York: Russell Sage Foundation.

Botvin, G. J. (2004). Advancing prevention science and practice: Challenges, critical issues, and future directions. *Prevention Science, 5*(1), 69–72.

Cashel, M. L. (2002). Child and adolescent psychological assessment: Current clinical practices and the impact of managed care. *Professional Psychology: Research and Practice, 33*(5), 446–453.

Castro, F. G., Barrera, M., & Martinez, C. R. (2004). The cultural adaptation of prevention interventions: Resolving tensions between fidelity and fit. *Prevention Science, 5*(1), 41–45.

Corrigan, P. W., Steiner, L., McCracken, S. G., Blaser, B., & Barr, M. (2001). Strategies for disseminating evidence-based practices to staff who treat people with serious mental illness. *Psychiatric Services, 52*(12), 1598–1606.

Feldman, R. A., & Wodarski, J. S. (1974). Bureaucratic constraints and methodological adaptations in community-based research. *American Journal of Community Psychology, 2,* 211–224.

Fischer, J., & Corcoran, K. (2007). *Measures for clinical practice and research: A sourcebook* (Vols. 1–2). New York: Oxford University Press.

Franklin, C., & Hopson, L. (2007). Facilitating the use of evidence-based practice in community organizations. *Journal of Social Work Education, 43*(3), 377–404.

Gambrill, E. (2006). Evidence-based practice and policy: Choices ahead. *Research on Social Work Practice, 16*(3), 338–357.

Glisson, C., & Hemmelgarn, A. (1998). The effects of organizational climate and interorganizational coordination on the quality of outcomes of children's service systems. *Child Abuse and Neglect, 22*(5), 401–421.

Glisson, C., & James, L. R. (2002). The cross-level effects of culture and climate in human services teams. *Journal of Organizational Behavior, 23,* 767–794.

Gosin, M. N., Dustman, A. E., Drapeau, A. E., & Harthun, M. L. (2003). Participatory Action Research: Creating an effective prevention curriculum for adolescents in the Southwestern U.S. *Health Education Research, 18*(3), 363–379.

Hecht, M. L., Marsiglia, F. F., Elek, E., Wagstaff, D. A., Kulis, S., & Dustman, P. (2003). Culturally grounded substance use prevention: An evaluation of the keepin' it REAL curriculum. *Prevention Science, 4*(4), 233–248.

Hemmelgarn, A. L., Glisson, C., & James, L. R. (2006). Organizational culture and climate: Implications for services and intervention research. *Clinical Psychology: Science and Practice, 13*(1), 75–89.

Hopson, L. M., & Wodarski, J. S. (2008). Guidelines and uses of rapid assessment instruments and the influence of managed care. In A. Roberts (Ed.), *Social worker's desk reference.* New York: Oxford University Press.

Hughes, J. (2003). Commentary: Participatory Action Research leads to sustainable school and community improvement. *School Psychology Review, 32*(1), 38–43.

Kelly, P. J. (2005). Practical suggestions for community interventions using Participatory Action Research. *Public Health Nursing, 22*(1), 65–73.

Kettlewell, P. W. (2004). Development, dissemination, and implementation of evidence-based treatments: Commentary. *Clinical Psychology: Science and Practice, 11*(2), 190–195.

Kidd, S. A., & Kral, M. J. (2005). Practicing participatory research. *Journal of Counseling Psychology, 52,* 187–195.

Kumpfer, K. L., Alvarado, R., Smith, P., & Bellamy, N. (2002). Cultural sensitivity and adaptation in family-based prevention interventions. *Prevention Science, 3*(3), 241–246.

Martinez-Brawley, E. E. (1995). Knowledge, diffusion, and transfer of technology: Conceptual premises and concrete steps for human services innovators. *Social Work, 40*(5), 670–684.

Miller, R. L. (2001). Innovation in HIV prevention: Organizational and intervention characteristics affecting program adoption. *American Journal of Community Psychology, 29,* 621–647.

Rittner, B., & Wodarski, J. S. (1995). Clinical assessment instruments in the treatment of child abuse and neglect. *Early Child Development and Care, 106,* 43–58.

Rohrbach, L. A., Grana, R., Sussman, S., & Valente, T. W. (2006). Type II translation: Transporting prevention interventions from research to real-world settings. *Evaluation in the Health Professions, 29*(3), 302–333.

Rubin, A., & Parrish, D. (2007). Views of evidence-based practice among faculty in MSW programs: A national survey. *Research on Social Work Practice, 17,* 110–122.

Schoenwald, S. K., & Hoagwood, K. (2001). Effectiveness, transportability, and dissemination of interventions: What matters when? *Psychiatric Services, 52*(9), 1190–1197.

Weissman, M. M., Verdeli, H., Gameroff, M. J., Bledsoe, S. E., Betts, K., Mufson, L., et al. (2006). A national survey of psychotherapy training in psychiatry, psychology, and social work. *Archives of General Psychiatry, 63*(8), 925–934.

Wood, J. M., Garb, H. N., Lilienfeld, S. O., & Nezworski, M. T. (2002). Clinical assessment. *Annual Review of Psychology, 53,* 519–543.

Index

About the Authors

John S. Wodarski is a professor of social work at The University of Tennessee. During his 30 years of experience as a research scientist, he has served as the principal investigator for projects that implement and evaluate evidence-based interventions and has successfully obtained funding for 75 federal, state, and foundation grants. He has coedited or coauthored over twenty books and teaches courses in research methods.

Laura M. Hopson is an assistant professor of social work at the University at Albany School of Social Welfare. Her research focuses on evidence-based prevention and intervention in schools and risk and protective factors associated with academic success. She teaches courses in advanced clinical practice and evaluation of clinical practice.

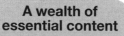